Goats

Their Care and Breeding
Ferial Rogers

Series Editor
Dennis Kelsey-Wood

K&R Books Ltd, Edlington
Horncastle, Lincs, England

First published 1979
by K & R Books Ltd
Edlington, Lincolnshire

ISBN 0 903264 36 6
Cover Photograph: British Toggenburg. Photo: C. Fairhurst

Typeset by Woolaston Parker Ltd and printed by Litho Letterpress Service, both of Leicester, England. Bound in Great Britain by Hunter & Foulis Ltd, of Edinburgh

Contents

Acknowledgements

My thanks are especially due to Lois Hetherington who has always been so ready, at any moment, to give me her unfailing help and advice. My thanks also to the following for their help and advice: the British Goat Society for their valuable information; Robert More for his general advice; Heather Birt who burnt the midnight oil to type the manuscript on time; Ronald Upson for reading the script; Bea Upson for supplying needlework and headstall patterns; Phyllis Minter for her excellent chapters (Breeding and Kidding, and Exhibiting); and finally Bill Bird, my right-hand man, whose extra effort gave me the time to write.

F. Rogers
Little Bealings
Suffolk 23.8.78

Publishers Acknowledgements

Whilst endorsing all of the above the publishers would like to extend their thanks to the following people – whose contribution did so much to help in the final preparation of this book. Mr and Mrs P. Spring for their untiring co-operation in making available goats for photographic sessions; the numerous people whose goats are featured in this book; Clifford Fairhurst for his superb colour photographs and for the problems these gave him; his wife Brenda for her patience with Cliff; Geoffrey Marsden for his valued advice and work; the author for her fine manuscript; and finally to the staff of the many companies whose joint efforts result in a book.

Chapter 1

Introduction and Brief History

'Thou shalt have goats milk enough for thy food for the good of thy household and for the maintenance of thy maidens' –

Solomon

The above quotation clearly shows that the goat has been with us for some considerable time as a producer of milk; indeed it may well have been amongst the very first animals domesticated, and selectively bred, by man.

In many regions of the world the goat still remains the prime source of milk, cheese, meat, and skins to numerous peoples – and none more so than those of nomadic inclinations – who traverse areas where cattle would find survival difficult due to harsh conditions.

It is the ability to obtain nourishment from almost barren land that has been the great strength, and appeal, of the goat to man right down the ages. Regarded generally as the poor man's cow the goat was more numerous in Roman Britain than the indigenous cattle; in many eastern countries man's wealth was based on the number of goats he owned. The goat can be found in Greek mythology as evidenced by the God of flocks and pastures – Pan – half man, half goat; it is found in astrology as the symbol of the zodiac Capricorn; became regarded as a sign of the devil and witchcraft in mediaeval times; and in our modern age many words are based on the latin for goat – *caper* – such words as caper itself, capricious, capriform, and so on.

Whilst always remaining popular in many parts of the world the goat did, in the west, acquire an undeserved stigma as we moved towards the 18th century; its owners were regarded as somewhat eccentric. This, however, was only one reason why it fell into decline for it must be remembered that, with rapid industrial advancement, more and more people moved away from the land whilst a corresponding increase in demand for leather, meat. and

5

milk, all favoured the cow with its much greater size.

The clock has more recently turned full circle for the escalation in the price of all cow products has brought about a revived interest in the keeping of goats; this is as it should be for they are a delightful animal that, given proper care, will reward their owners with not only by-products but with much enjoyment.

In order to have a better appreciation of the goat it is perhaps as well to consider, from the outset, exactly what a goat is and in what respects it differs from its relatives, who these are, and how they are grouped.

What is a Goat?

In zoological terminology the European goat is called *Capra hircus*. The use of Latin for the naming of animals has been arrived at as a result of international agreement; it enables people from different countries to readily identify any given animal – which would be most difficult if this were not the case. Each individual animal that will freely breed with a similar animal of the opposite sex, and produce fertile offspring, is called a species; and a number of very similar species are grouped together into what is called a genus. Thus there are a number of goats in the genus *Capra* but only one European goat *hircus*. The scientific name of any animal is denoted by the use of both the generic and specific names together; this system is called the binomial system of nomenclature and is based on the original works of a Swedish naturalist called Carl Linnaeus, who, in 1758, published the 10th edition of his now famous work *Systema Naturae.*

No animal has a single diagnostic feature, therefore it is placed in a genera on the basis of a number of such, which may be morphological or biological, and which it shares with other animals. Goats are characterised by having horns which sweep upwards and away from the head after the style of a scimitar. The males possess beards and a very marked odour known to most people who come into contact with them. They are of medium size ranging from 63 cm. in *C. nubiana* to 110 cm. in *C. falconeri*. In range of distribution goats are found in Europe, Asia, and North Africa: it will be remembered that we are at this time discussing the wild goat and not the domestic goat which is, of course, found throughout the world. The skull of the goat has certain special features which distinguish it from its close relative the sheep (genus Ovis) but the two are indeed very closely related. Sheep have no beards, no obvious odour, and possess horns which typically curve forward. There have been numerous instances of matings between goats and sheep but as far as is known such off-spring that have resulted never attained maturity. Berry (1938) gives the chromosome count of the goat as 60 (domestic) and the sheep as 54 with hybrids having 57.

Goats, Sheep, Chamois, Muskox, and others, are grouped in the sub-family *Caprinae* which in turn is one of five such divisions of the family *Bovidae*. This family is of the utmost importance to man for in it are found all wild cattle (the ancestors to our modern breeds) as well as Antilopes, Hartebeests, Gnus, and such.

Features of the family are paired, unbranched, true horns carried by either or both sexes and which are not shed; no incisor or canine teeth, which have been replaced by a hard plate; and lateral toes which are vestiges or absent. Each of these features is therefore a feature of the goat. *Bovidae* is itself one of five families which come together to form the sub-order *Ruminantia* – a vast group containing an immense number of animals – which, apart from those already mentioned, also includes Giraffes, Deer, and Pronghorns. Features of the group are: modified lower jaw canines which act as incisors; horns which may be solid (antlers) or hollow (as in the goat); and of course a modified stomach, including the *rumen,* from which the group takes its name. The features of the sub-order are again features of the goat and it is worth mentioning the way in which rumination, in essence, works.

The stomach is divided into four compartments; food is passed into the first two, the *rumen* and the *reticulum*, for partial digestion before being regurgitated for further mastication after which it

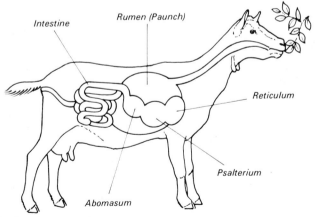

The digestive system of a goat.

passes into the *psalterium* and the *abomasum* to complete the digestive cycle. The advantage of this system is that the animal may consume food, initially, at a faster rate than if it were to spend long periods masticating. It is then able to move to more protective covering, if required, where it can consume its food at greater leisure. Goats may move down a mountain to gather their needs and return to higher, more inaccessible spots to 'chew the cud'.

It should be stated that Chevrotains (Mouse Deer), which are in this group, have only three compartments to their stomach but full rumination still takes place.

The ruminants are one of three sub-orders that comprise the order Artiodactyla – which is as far as we need to consider in relation to the goat. The members of this order include Pigs, Camels, and Hippos, in addition to those already mentioned. The prime features of the order are that they are even-toed hoofed (Ungulate) mammals in which the toes are encased in a hard bony covering. Only two toes are normally present and used for walking on – the exception being the Hippopotamus.

Most members of the group are herbivorous (principally vegetation eaters), the Pigs and Peccaries being omniverous; all are terrestrial with the exception of the Hippos. The goat shows all of the typical features of the group so that we have now covered all the principle features of a goat which may be summarized as follows: even-toed ungulate, herbivorous, terrestrial, a ruminant with modified dentition; hollow horns growing over a solid core arising from the skull, and unbranched with a scimitar-style backward curve; possess beards in the male; a typical odour; and are medium sized animals highly developed to survive in arid conditions.

Development of the domestic goat

The above brief look at the wild goat gives us a general picture of a *typical* goat, but of course domesticated varieties show certain modifications which have come about through man's desire to improve the animal to better suit his needs. It is generally accepted that the ancestor of the domestic goat was the Persian Wild Goat (*Capra h. aegagrus*) which ranged from Greece through Persia and Asia Minor. Of reddish-brown body colour, with white underparts and long sweeping horns, it is a far cry from the pure-bred specimens we see today; yet the rugged character of this wild ancestor has been retained. As successive waves of peoples invaded western Europe so they brought with them their way of living, and their livestock, which – over many

8

centuries – became established. As goats were, in the west, predominantly owned by the poorer classes, selective breeding took place only at a very slow pace and the goat was of course an all purpose animal; milk yields were by no means comparable to that found today. There were – and still are – countless types of goats found throughout the world and it has only been during the last century that *breed* development has taken place on a carefully programmed basis.

It is clear that milk yield in the tundra of arid desert regions would not compare with that of temperate climates found in Europe and the USA. It is not surprising to find therefore that it was from these regions that the basic breeds of today would evolve. Switzerland, with its lush meadows, is credited with being the home of the modern dairy goat and, from stocks obtained from that country, breeders have steadily improved a number of breeds. As a result of the success of imported goats numerous indigenous types have faded from the scene and goats such as the Old English, and Welsh, no longer exist.

There are two goats whose hair is their main claim to fame – the Angora and the Cashmere – both require certain climatic conditions to be successful. Although most goats in the world are basically kept for meat and then milk it is a fact that, as meat producers, there is no recognized type in Britain or the USA as both concentrate on milk yield.

The formation of the British Goat Society in 1879 heralded a big step forward for goat improvement; the opening of the Herd book in 1886 was another positive move. Organized shows have become increasingly popular and serve to promote goatkeeping, whilst many clubs and societies have, over the years, further encouraged careful breeding. Certainly any person contemplating keeping a goat is well advised to contact a local society and become a member.

Sadly, a number of people live under the illusion that a goat will replace their lawn mower and to such people I would say that they will be quickly disillusioned for nothing is further from the truth. A goat requires as much love and affection as any other animal and he also needs due care and consideration. It is an old, well-worn, cliche that we learn by our mistakes and there is no doubt of the truth of this. If, in the light of my own experience, I can benefit aspiring new goatkeepers in helping them to avoid the pitfalls I encountered then this small handbook will have been well justified.

Chapter 2

The Breeds

Unlike the natural species a breed is controlled by man who can therefore select those features which are most desirable. Thus, he can breed purely for a given colour, for size, milk yield, or whatever, to the exclusion of natural selection. Though zoologically *Capra hircus* was at the end of the natural system of goats, from it have been bred many specific races, or breeds, which thus form another system controlled by man. We see a similar situation in dogs where the species *Canis familiaris* has been developed into countless pure breeds.

Of the many breeds of goats found throughout the world most are of no immediate interest to the western goatkeeper for they are seen only locally in their country of origin. A number that have, however, become established include those of most interest to European and American keepers. We shall consider the main breeds: the Saanen, British Saanen, Toggenburg, British Toggenburg, Anglo-Nubian, and British Alpine. Coverage will also be given to the Golden Guernsey.

The Saanen and Toggenburgs were imported into Britain in the early years of this century and are well established as pure breeds. Where, however, they were crossed with native stock the resulting progeny were prefixed by 'British' to indicate that though they might have been of pedigree stock they were not pure-bred. Goats which are cross-bred over the whole range of pedigree breeds are said to be simply 'British'.

Goats which closely resemble the various pure breeds but whose pedigree is complete enough for them to be eligible into the Herd book must have the word 'type' after their name; 'Saanen type' or 'Toggenburg type'.

The Saanen

This all-white goat originated in Switzerland and is the most popular of the milk producers. It has a short silky coat and may be horned or hornless. The ears are medium size and carried erect and forward. The neck is long and slender and females may carry beards, and tassels, but these are not considered essentials. Weight approximately 56–77 kg. according to sex. The Saanen has a most agreeable, placid, temperament which makes it ideal for free range or stall feeding. Milk yield is high and it has a long lactation period. The British Saanen is somewhat larger than its Swiss counterpart and this is believed to stem from a number of early importations from Holland which were of this type.

A British goatling (Langham Leila, B.I.S. twice) seen at eighteen months old. Owner Miss P. V. Minter.

British Saanen

Of Saanen type; these goats could easily be mistaken for pure Saanen and differ only in being somewhat larger, having a weight range of 63–99 kg., and as such are the heaviest of the breeds being considered. Though officially the points of the British Saanen are the same as for its pure namesake it is, generally, longer legged and longer in the head. Milk yield is the highest of the milk goats and lactation the longest so it could justifiably be considered as an improved version of the Saanen. It is bred with conformation and milk yield being of greater importance than type.

The Toggenburg
Another Swiss breed which for some years competed with the Saanen for yield but did not keep pace with others and, as a result, has lost some of its popularity. None the less it is still a good producer and in make up has few faults. Colour is from fawn to chocolate – with white or fawn markings down the nose, on the ear tips, down the back, round the rump, and under the tail. It is a small breed with a weight range of 57–70 kg. depending on sex. Outside of the UK the breed has achieved better yield and it is to be hoped that this fine breed will continue to prosper with the introduction of imported blood.

Toggenburg. Photo: Diane Pearce.

British Toggenburg
Larger than its pure namesake, it was evolved by crossings of the parent breed with other goats of mixed Swiss origin. The colour and markings are as for its parents but tend to be darker. Type may

vary a little and the coat is shorter than in the pure breed. It is a good milk producer and enjoys growing popularity. Weight range 63–79 kg. according to sex.

Anglo-Nubian

This is the oldest of the breeds in Britain and was evolved by crossing native stock with imported animals from the east. It is instantly recognizable with its lop ears, Roman nose, and often patch work colour pattern of caramel, red, black, and brown – though it can be of any colour. Although called Nubian many of the early imports came from Egypt, Abyssinia, and as far as India. The breed has retained its characteristic looks in spite of no fresh imports for over half a century. Faults include wry nose and twisted tail, the former being considered the more objectionable though both are hereditary and go back to the original imports. In stance it is very different from the Swiss breed and holds its head high and, as it has high hips, this is invariably accompanied by a dipped back. Hind legs are straight and free from any sign of 'cow-hocks'. It is somewhat noisier than the Swiss breed; when mated to them its nose and ear features are transmitted. Butterfat content of Anglo-Nubian milk is higher than in any other breed, this is the goat for quality rather than quantity. Weight range, 54–72 kg. in females, males weigh more.

Anglo-Nubian. Photo: Diane Pearce.

British Alpine

A breed developed in England, it is in essence a black and white Toggenburg though it can be of slightly larger size and weight. Saanen blood has been used in its make-up: facially it should have the normal Swiss markings as in the Toggenburg. The Alpine can look a most impressive animal and deserves the high popularity it has gained.

British Alpine. Photo: Diane Pearce.

Golden Guernsey

As its name suggests this goat is from the Channel Isles. Several years ago it was all but extinct and endeavours are now being made to preserve, and build up, its numbers. A trust was set up in the Isles and selective breeding with mainland stock has been carefully programmed; it is hoped its future is now secure.

The most notable characteristic of the breed is obviously its true golden colour. However, a colour range from weak tea to ginger is permissible, but there should be no white markings. The ears are erect, the face dished, and the neck is long; the hair may be long or short and the stature is small and fine-boned. Milking qualities should prove to be very adequate. The breed is gaining considerable support and is on the list of the Rare Breeds Survival Trust and also has its own breed society – The English Golden Guernsey Goat Society. The breed has not yet been officially recognized by the British Goat Society but this important body has opened a register for pure-bred stock and after a trial period a herd book will be opened.

Lactation Periods

Animals from temperate zones will be found to breed according to the seasons; they mate in the autumn when the days become shorter and the young are produced in the spring, as the weather turns warmer. In equatorial regions, where the days stay much the same throughout the year, animals are not so subject to such clearly defined cycles and they can breed more often. This may account for the long lactations of goats from the northern regions and the corresponding shorter ones of the Nubian types, whose origins are in the Middle East.

'Nannies and Billies'

We will end this chapter with this point of terminology. The use of Nanny and Billy goat for female and male is well established, though as long ago as 1885 Holmes Pegler took exception to this. He was pleased to note, however, that a trend towards the American terms of Doe and Buck was gaining popularity: his optimism was to be unfounded and goats are still commonly described with the old terms. It is, therefore, worth pointing out that Doe and Buck is the official – and correct – way to describe female and male goats.

Chapter 3

Purchasing a Goat

Practical considerations

Before rushing out and acquiring the first appealing kid you can lay your hands on, it would be of greater value if you were to spend the time considering the problems and viability of goatkeeping. It is always wise to deliberate a little extra when purchasing animals. If they cannot be maintained adequately it is they who suffer most, whilst the well-intentioned owner might also find he has a few problems if that animal is a goat.

The very qualities that have made goats so successful in the wild might not be so well appreciated by the new owner who did

Miss P. V. Minter seen with Mayflower Mary and her triplet kids.

not ponder enough on these aspects. For example, we have established that the goat can survive on almost anything and is therefore not averse to trying all of your flowers – or anything else that might come her way, whether this be your shopping bag and contents, or the children's toys. The goat is very, very accomplished at scaling the impossible and maybe your neighbour's garden looks more inviting than yours. Are you able to contain the goat and can you live with an animal who has more curiosity than the proverbial cat?

The 'back to the land and self-sufficiency idea' may look good on TV and bring pictures of a promise of a richer life, which it certainly can do, but it also means mucking out on cold damp winter days. All of that healthy fresh milk will not arrive by itself and must be collected morning and evening, seven days a week, fair weather or foul. Housing must be kept in good repair and the fencing will need attention too; will your pets like their new companions and do all of the household want a goat? If you do not keep on top of things then how does your wife or husband feel about a few mice moving in – still want a goat?

If you have not by now given up the desire to have one of these charming young ladies, then might I suggest you have two. Goats are gregarious creatures and, with this in view, it is really better to consider starting with two animals so that they will have companionship. The owner of one goat will have to be prepared to spend more time with her to make up for the lack of other goats. As she usually lives in harmony with other animals, she could derive some companionship from pets of the household.

Often euphemistically described as the 'backyard goat' two animals should need rather less room than one cow; they will also be more economical to keep. It is a law of nature that the smaller the unit, the larger the output in relation to the expenditure of energy, therefore, for what is spent in feed, there should be greater return in produce. This, of course, will depend on care being taken in providing a sensible diet.

It must be stressed that however lovable, and however much of pets they might be, goats are livestock and should be treated in accordance with the needs of livestock. Only the eccentric few would have you believe otherwise (and these, unfortunately, receive rather more publicity than is desirable) and this can only be of detriment to the goat. Nevertheless, it is possible to keep goats intensively in a back garden. As they will have to be stall-fed, extra care must be taken in ensuring that they are given a well balanced diet. It is desirable that some sort of provision is made for exercising and, as already hinted, due consideration should be given to neighbours. The cleaning routine must be carried out regularly and efficiently; muck heaps should not be allowed to grow too big or spread too wide. These criteria will, of course, apply in whatever environment the goat is kept. Obviously, the more land you have at your disposal the better, and a smallholding would be ideal. It is often possible to convert an old barn or out-building, if structurally sound, into a very efficient goathouse. If the goat has access to a well fenced paddock this will be a considerable advantage or, failing this, perhaps a yard attached to the goat house could be provided. Tethering is not to be recommended although some people do: in any case, a goat that is tethered should be kept under strict surveillance and should be moved twice a day.

Given adequate feeding and housing, and treated with the respect and affection which they deserve, they will reward you well. You will have a ready supply of milk and the surplus can be made into butter and cheese; in addition there will always be a ready supply of manure for your crops.

When considering the possibilities of your scheme you could well broaden your field of vision by making the acquaintance of existing goatkeepers in your area. It would make sound sense to become a member of a local goat club; there would then be ample opportunity to speak to someone with experience on any point on

British Toggenburg kid at five weeks old.

which you would like more information. In addition, you could attend club meetings and shows. The British Goat Society will be very happy to supply the name and address of the secretary of your nearest local club.

The Next Step

When you have decided that you are well equipped to provide for the needs of a goat, then is the time to think about which animal will suit you best. It is better that you make your first purchase from a reputable breeder to ensure good stock with known parentage.

Be prepared to pay for something worthwhile and, for reasons already stated, do try to have more than one animal. Extra time spent on caring for two goats is negligible and one more will take up little extra room; one animal will be very lonely without any companionship and, when confined to close quarters, will probably make a lot more noise and upset the neighbours. Two goats from a good quality herd should serve you well.

What Age to Buy?

An advantage will be gained by buying a milking goat because you will have a supply of milk immediately. In this case it would be helpful to have one or two practice milkings under the watchful eye of an experienced handler first. A goat in her second or third lactation should have the greatest potential yield and be more stable than a first kidder. An in-kid goatling might seem to be an expediency because she is young and she will have time to settle in before you start to milk her. It must be remembered, however, that being milked is as new an experience for her as it is for you; this might give rise to a little difficulty until you have both mastered the new situation.

A kid, while the cheapest to buy, will be more expensive because it will be perhaps eighteen months before she gives you any milk. Nonetheless, you will have lots of time to become acquainted and build a happy relationship together. With two milking goats, a constant supply of milk can be assured. As most goats will milk for at least two years, each can be bred in alternate years. Bearing this in mind, a mature milker who has recently kidded, and a year old goatling who is ready to breed, would make a good combination for the potential new owner to seek.

Favoured Breed

No doubt you have a preference for a certain breed. The Saanen type is generally placid and affectionate but best suited to free range; the Toggenburg type is the same, but probably not quite so placid. Alpines, although very friendly, have an independent nature and might need to be ruled with a firm hand, also they are noted for being able to scale quite high fences. Anglo-Nubians are very intelligent and produce milk of the finest quality but they can be exceedingly noisy. Guernseys are small and sweet natured and probably adapt better than the other types to being kept on a small scale, though it must be remembered that they will still need exercise. While it is perfectly true that some breeds adapt to certain environments better than others, this is by no means always the case, or the only criteria.

Physical Character

More important than the breed is the quality of the animal that you wish to buy; it behoves you well to become accustomed as to what constitutes a worthy animal.

A good goat must be deeper at the hind quarters than the chest, but the chest should be broad enough to ensure a strong heart and fine fettle. When viewed from above, the goat should be

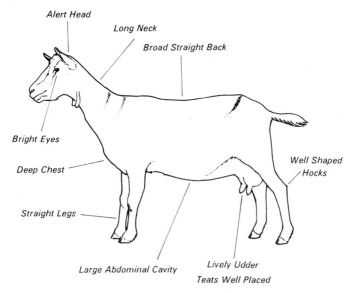

Alert Head

Long Neck

Broad Straight Back

Bright Eyes

Deep Chest

Straight Legs

Well Shaped Hocks

Large Abdominal Cavity

Lively Udder
Teats Well Placed

Points of a good goat.

Anglo-Nubian kid. This breed can show many coat colours and markings.

wedge shaped, being slim at the shoulders and widening out towards the rump. The abdominal cavity should be large, and the ribs deep to accommodate the ample stomach. The back should be straight with a slight downwards tendency towards the rear and the back legs should be wide set to accommodate the udder. The legs should all be straight with no tendency towards cow-hocks.

The udder need not necessarily be large to ensure a good milk supply, but it must be supple and lively. The teats should be neat, placed fairly well apart, and taper forward, in fact they should have a look of being placed on afterwards. The neck should be long and the head held high; the animal should be alert and carry herself well. The eyes should be bright and the gums a healthy pink; the coat should look clean, bright, and well cared for. These points should ensure a strong well balanced animal with a healthy constitution.

It is better to avoid a squat goat with a shallow frame and a small abdominal cavity. A large udder might be more flesh than milk vessels and it will be more vulnerable to injury. Fetlocks which point inwards will cause the goat to walk badly, and her feet will become mis-shapen. Possible points towards an unhealthy goat are general lethargy, a staring coat and dull eyes, the gums might be pallid and the breath offensive.

A thin goat is not necessarily an unhealthy goat. It is not in a goats physiology to be fat therefore a thin, but otherwise bright and lively animal, is 'milking off her back'. This means that her good energy output is being converted into milk rather than fat. Be watchful if you want to buy a very large goat; marked broadness across her back might mean that she has too much fat round her kidneys and this is not a good point.

The Unknown Quantity

A goat's age can be generally ascertained by looking at her teeth – she will have her full complement of 32 at one year old. These will consist of eight incisors in the lower jaw plus six molars on either side of the lower and upper jaws. These will grow to full maturity by the time she is five years old. At about six to seven years the teeth will start to wear down. However, this will only serve as a rough guide, as a goat with really well worn teeth could have been used to barking trees on rough pasture land.

If you decide to buy a goat which has no known parentage, but you examine the animal first with an intelligent and critical eye, it might be possible to get a bargain. It might also be an interesting exercise to use this goat as a foundation in grading up a small pedigree herd of your own.

Be that as it may, if you buy from a reputable breeder you will be surer of what you are procuring. You will know the goat's ancestry and this will help you to ascertain her milking qualities.

Individual Character

Each goat will have a personality of her own, and this is a point that should not be overlooked when selecting an animal. A goat who is used to free range might well be unhappy when confined to close quarters. Should you live in a built-up area, a particularly vociferous animal will not enhance your reputation with the neighbours. My own goats are out of neighbours' earshot and I remember the evening when I had a phone call from a friend in a state of agitation. Her goats are kept in her long and adequate back garden but she is quite close to neighbours. That particular morning she had taken delivery of a goat who had spent the rest of the day shouting at the top of her very raucous voice; she was also pacing about wildly and threatening to do structural damage to the goathouse. She was upsetting the neighbours and my friend asked me to take her and house her in my very solid old stable until a new home could be found for her.

She was a very young goat and she did indeed resemble a

howling banshee. Through an unfortunate set of circumstances but through nobody's fault she had had several moves and was highly nervous. However, she settled down into my system and is with me still; her name is Chantelle and she can be the most dreadful bully, so she needs to be handled firmly.

The Male Goat

It is not advisable for the first time owner to keep a male, but I feel that he is worthy of a few paragraphs to explain the reasons why.

Most breeders feel that a male goat is not worth his keep unless they have several females to justify him service. Even then, they take great pains to ensure that they only select a really top rate animal. It is much better for a small owner to transport the in-season female to the stud male when the time comes.

Pure Saanen male goat. Owner Mrs. F. Davies.

Popular belief is that all goats smell and the male is responsible for this inglorious distinction – it is certainly true that in the rutting season his scent can be strong and evil.

A castrated male will not smell and there was a time when these goats had a useful role to play as draft animals. Perhaps a castrated male will make a friendly pet, but all too often he will be bought by uninformed humans who believe the fallacy that he will keep the grass down.

A castrated male as a pet will still need to be fed and housed properly; he will grow strong and need adequate housing and fencing. The consequences of his blundering through to next door's garden and vandalising their vegetable patch do not bear thinking of. Their year's supply of produce destined for the deep freeze could be consumed or trampled on in one go. In this case, perhaps the deep freeze would be the best place for him.

A male as a pet will surely be more trouble than a dog and these poor goats are often doomed to spend a miserable and lonely life on the end of a tether.

I do know one young couple who keep a stud male and no other goats; he is properly registered with the British Goat Society and in the breeding season he works. His constant companion is a dog and his owners love him. Bearing cost and return in mind, they do not make any money out of him and neither do they expect to. However, it must be stressed that these people are very unusual and this is not really to be recommended.

Chapter 4

Housing and Pasturing

Basic Structure of House

Goats do not need a palace in which to live providing that which they do have is warm in winter, well ventilated, not draughty, and is of sufficient size to enable them to move about freely. One hears of goats housed in tiny chicken huts and outside lavatories but really neither of these are adequate. While it might be out of the question for you to have the perfect goathouse, there are several basic principles which can be incorporated in the layout of the buildings.

Adequate ventilation is vital to ensure the good health of the herd, and slats in the roof to aid the escape of foul air would be ideal. Alternatively, air bricks or in the case of wooden buildings, louvre boards, could be fitted near the eaves. Windows with a southerly aspect which can be opened hopper-fashion, should make a light airy place. Stable doors should be fitted so that the top half can be open if the goats need to be in when the weather is bad.

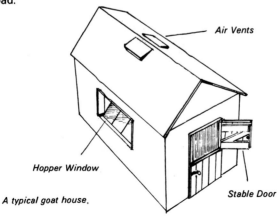

Air Vents

Hopper Window

A typical goat house.

Stable Door

Goats in the wild will make their sleeping places on thick beds of bracken in well sheltered locations; here they will be snug, comfortable, and dry with never the hint of a draught. It is equally important that there are no draughts in the sleeping quarters of the domestic goat if she is to remain fit and healthy.

Existing Buildings

It is often possible to convert existing out-buildings into a very adequate goathouse. Lucky is the person who has an old out-building made of stone. These old places were often built with walls a foot thick, thus ensuring they stayed warm in winter and cool in summer. Alternatively, an old stable with the hayrack lowered would probably be tailor-made for the job. Part of an old barn or a garage, so long as they are structurally sound, might serve your purpose well.

A New House

In the absence of any existing buildings, it would surely be sound sense to spend as much as you could afford on providing a goathouse with a good solid outer framework. Wooden pre-fabricated sheds can be bought in a variety of sizes and instructions for building on site are issued with the kits. Even so, it might be optimistic to expect any but the most competent 'do-it-yourselfer' to accomplish this without some sort of professional assistance.

Old Nissen huts become available sometimes, and these, together with other likely structures, can be found at special auction sales. With this in mind it is a good idea to keep an eye on the auctioneers announcements in the local press. Should you elect for a corrugated iron structure remember that it will be subject to extremes of temperature, therefore, some extra insulation might be advisable. This could take the form of padded sacks battened onto the roof.

Without a doubt, the finest new goathouse of all would be that built with bricks. Unfortunately, bricks are so expensive that they are way out of reach of the pockets of all but a few. However, breeze-blocks should make a perfectly adequate alternative.

The Outer Yard

Some stockmen consider an earth floor to be more natural and this is known as a hot-bed; goats rely on a steady build-up of litter to keep them warm and the urine should be absorbed to a great extent in the litter. The land, however, must be such that it allows for drainage of excess moisture. If managed properly and kept within sensible proportions, the goats bed should always be clean and sweet smelling; the manure from this type of bedding is considered to be of a superior quality because of the high nitrogen content.

It is generally accepted though, that a concrete floor is better. This should be well insulated with a thick layer of hardcore base and the concrete surface should fall gently to a drainage point, which can take the form of a small channel running in front of the pens and leading to a drain covered with a grating. Thus, the goathouse should be clean and dry and the outside surrounding area can be well maintained.

The Interior

Having disposed of the question of the outside structure your mind can be applied to the design of the interior of the building. Firstly, take into account the ease of the handler as well as the needs of the goat. Several people with large herds house their goats on an open plan system in the same way that cows or sheep might be kept. However, sheep and cows will live amicably together whereas goats will not. They establish a hierarchy in which the strong will dominate the weaker members of the herd; for this reason it is much more usual, and strongly recommended, to have a loose-box for each animal.

The Loose-Box (Pen)

The minimum floor space should be 5' × 5' (1·5 × 1·5 m.) and the sides should be about 4 feet high (1·2 m). This should be high enough to stop the goat from jumping out but at the same time facilitate the companionship of the other animals. Goats can become remarkably adept in undoing catches on doors, and this is worth taking into account when you make your choice of fastenings – remember, however, that it should be easy enough for you to open without difficulty. A bolt with an under catch could be placed about one third of the way down the door.

Inside the Loose-Box

Goats like to raise themselves up by the forefeet when looking over the pen and some sort of stand could be provided for this. I use pieces of rock in my pens because I feel that, in some small way, this helps to keep the feet in trim.

Kids like to jump, and their pens should have a box for this purpose. Placed on its side, the box will double up as a little sleeping house.

A hayrack must be provided but do not use haynets as they can be dangerous. Water and other foods can be given in buckets which are slotted into iron holders, and these can be purchased from farm suppliers. Alternatively, buckets can be hung on a hook with the aid of baler twine; this can be made stronger and more permanent if three pieces are plaited together and mineral licks can be hung up in the same fashion. A hayrack and manger combined should be easy to construct.

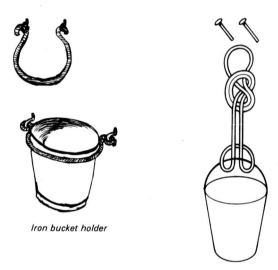

Iron bucket holder

Bucket hanging with binder twine and Nails

Goats are notoriously wasteful and they are quite likely to pull as much hay on to the floor as they eat, so in the interests of economy a hayrack with a double front could be built.

Many breeders favour the method of feeding from outside the pen and in such cases the door has an opening for the goat's head, and a bucket is slotted in an iron frame beneath this. Branches can be tied up with baler twine using a slip knot, but do remember to move these immediately after use.

Stealing

Eating arrangements should not allow one goat to reach over and steal another's food. I have a double rack over two pens which are used to house my goats Chantelle and Aphrodite; I would go into the goathouse in the evenings to find Aphrodite's half of the rack empty while Chantelle's was quite full. I became increasingly

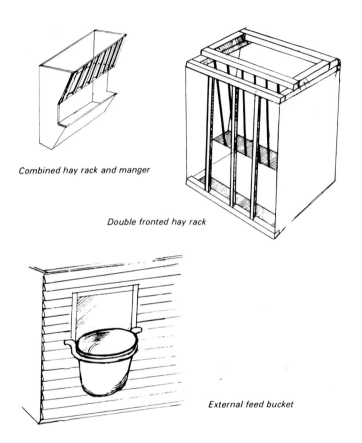

Combined hay rack and manger

Double fronted hay rack

External feed bucket

aware that, while Chantelle wore a smug and self-satisfied expression, Aphrodite was looking increasingly more despondent. The awful truth that Chantelle was stealing Aphrodite's hay dawned on me. The situation was remedied by putting Aphrodite's hay in the far corner of her pen – well out of Chantelle's reach – and now Chantelle has the whole rack to herself. No doubt she still feels that she is stealing from Aphrodite and everybody is happy.

Other Features of the House

Do try to have a running water supply and adequate lighting for winter evenings if you can. The gangway should be wide enough to accommodate a barrow as this will make mucking out much easier.

It is far better to keep the food bins and hay under the same roof as your goats and you will fully appreciate this when the weather is cold and wet. A separate milking parlour would be very desirable but not within the scope of many; nonetheless, it is important that the goats are removed from their pens to be milked and a raised bench for a goat to stand on will make this easier. It is suggested that the milking bench is placed in a corner with the food container on your right and a clasp fixed in front, so that any difficult goat can be tied up.

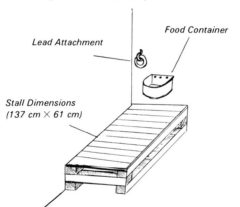

Food Container

Lead Attachment

Stall Dimensions
(137 cm × 61 cm)

A typical milking bench

The Muck Heap

The smell of a muck heap, whilst acceptable in a country district, is unlikely to meet with approval in towns. The heap should be kept as neat as possible and within sensible proportions. It should be located in a fairly secluded spot, but be near enough to the goathouse to minimize labour when cleaning out. Here it can rot down into high quality manure for your garden; any excess can be offered to neighbours which is bound to win you favour. A smallholder's tractor fitted with a scoop would be ideal for mucking out purposes, but most of us have to rely on the fork, shovel, and wheelbarrow.

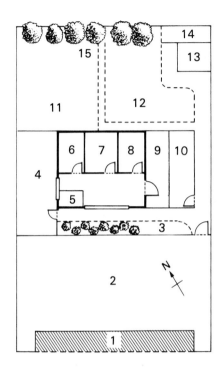

Goathouse in back garden

1 House	9 Covered way
2 Ornamental garden	10 Exercise yard
3 Fruit bushes	11 Goat garden
4 Other livestock	12 Kitchen garden
5 Milking stool	13 Tool shed
6 Pen 1	14 Compost heap
7 Pen 2	15 Fruit trees
8 Food store	

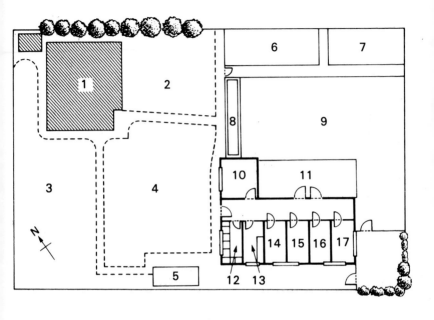

Goathouse in country garden

1 House
2 Kitchen garden
3 Flower garden
4 Goat garden
5 Tool shed
6, 7 Other livestock
8 Hay and branches rack
9 Exercise yard
10 Hay and food store
11 Covered area
12 Food store
13 Milking pen
14 Spare pen
15 Pen 1
16 Pen 2
17 Pen 3

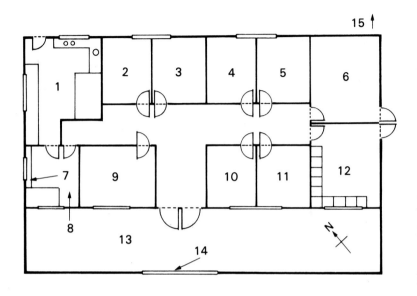

Goathouse on smallholding

1 Dairy (with equipment)	9 Kids pen
2 Pen 1	10 Pen 6
3 Pen 2	11 Pen 5
4 Pen 3	12 Food store
5 Pen 4	13 Shelter
6 Hay store	14 Gate to paddock
7 Medicine shelf	15 To house and plantation
8 Milking parlour	

Yarding

Even in the very smallest set-up a small exercise yard will be an advantage. Goats are by nature playful creatures so perhaps you could provide a few toys for them. The ground can be kept clean by scraping down with a hoe and it must be done often; you might prefer to concrete the yard and this can be swept down every day. Do remember though, that in play, the goats will be apt to slip and slide and they could easily hurt their knees or bruise their udders.

Simple play equipment for goats

Leading

If you have only two goats and no yarding facilities, you could put aside an hour each day to take them out on a lead. Be prepared to amble along so that they can browse amongst the hedgerows as you go.

Should you acquire a goat who has not been trained to it, she might be difficult to lead and it will be fruitless to pull back on the lead as the goat tugs forward. Indeed, constriction of the neck can bring on a partial collapse in the goat and she will fall quivering to the ground. For anybody not prepared for this to happen, it can be an alarming experience and it is best to leave her and she will recover quickly. In these circumstances it might be better for you to use a halter and this can be made at home with 2 yards (1·8 m) of rope.

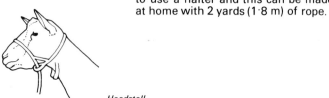

Headstall

Tying Together

I once heard it stated on a radio programme that in the absence of adequate penning two goats could be tied together for exercise. Their natural contrariness would make each want to go in the opposite direction and in this way they would not get into mischief. One just cannot believe this and I am quite sure that no person of authority would ever recommend it. If one goat were to jump a fence, she would be strangled for sure.

Tethering

If you have to do this then make sure that the tethering pin is of a revolving type, so that the goat can move around freely without winding herself up. Move her twice a day and always keep her in view as on the end of a tether a goat is in a very vulnerable position; she has no way of escape and might become the butt of taunts from small children.

I know one goat who has been tethered for eight years and so was well used to it, but, one day, she was suddenly startled and became entangled in the hedgerow and strangled before anyone got to her. I heard of another goat which was tethered on common land and the brush caught fire and she died. It can be mentioned that the Anglo-Nubians in particular resent any type of tethering and this should be borne in mind if purchasing this breed.

Open Pasture

The paddock where the goats can roam free is ideal, and the more bushes and undergrowth there are on site the better. If the land can be strip-grazed this will not only stop the ground becoming 'goat-starved' but also stem the build up of worm infestation. The land is divided into two, or even better, three strips; as each strip becomes tired so the goats can be moved to the next, and so on. This will allow the land a period for new growth, and also keep worm infestation down to a minimum. One strip at a time could be given a dose of fertilizer and reseeded with a herbal hay prepared specially for goats. You could have a soil sample tested by the Ministry of Agriculture to see what is needed in the way of fertilizer.

In the absence of any existing fencing, 5 feet high (1·5 m) pig-netting, strung between concrete posts about 4 yards (3·6 m) apart, is strong and serviceable, but very costly. An electric fence is cheaper and might well be the answer. Never use barbed wire because the goats could hurt themselves quite badly if they touch the barbs.

If you have a paddock do make sure that the goats have

somewhere to go when it rains. A very simple structure should be quite adequate and you could probably make use of materials which you already have. For ours we used four solid wooden posts, 2 old pallets, 3 old doors, and an old roll of asbestos. The pallets had pieces of wood tacked over the back to cover the gaps and were used for the back of the structure. The doors were used for the roof and these were covered with the asbestos.

Makeshift out-door shelter

Do discourage people from feeding your animals as you never know what they might throw to them. This will also put unnecessary strain on the fences as the goats reach over to where they know there is a likely source of titbits. For goats, 'the grass on the other side is always greener' and a piece of succulent pasture just beyond the bounds of the paddock can play havoc with the fencing.

I had just such a hazard in the form of an enormous blackberry thicket. A considerable amount of time and effort was spent in re-routing the fence to bring the thicket within the boundary. The goats have lost interest in the thicket now and transferred their attentions to a piece of elm hedge farther up. Are not 'forbidden fruits' always the more succulent?

A particularly badly behaved kid might become remarkably adept at getting through quite small gaps in the fencing. As an emergency measure you could try using a yoke.

A simple yoke

Chapter 5

Feeding

Modern scientific study of various animals' metabolism and special dietary needs has neglected the goat to a great extent. Nevertheless, what research has been done has tutored well on the various nutrients which are essential to the health of our stock. Old herdsmen know nothing of such things, but after a lifetime with their animals they have an intrinsic knowledge of their needs and they come up with much the same answers as the scientists.

If we could observe goats foraging in the wild we would have a valuable insight into what they like to eat and what is of most dietary value to them. Fine grass and clover will be ignored as they look for the stalky fibrous plants; succulent tops are nipped out from amongst the bracken and the heather. Marshlands will provide an abundance of herbs that will not be found in an upland meadow. Tree bark provides an excellent source of food, although many domestic goat owners know this to their cost. In winter the goats must forage for roots when green stuff is scarce. They have a wide and varied palate, but they are very fastidious and they like their food to be clean and of the highest quality. We can also observe that chewing the cud brings them great contentment and it is vital to their mental stability.

In the wild then, goats should be well able to provide themselves with an adequate diet but domestic goats must usually have their food provided for them. Goat owners are responsible for ensuring that their goat's diet is well balanced.

We have all heard of the proverbial 'gallon milker' and many new goat owners are disappointed when their new charges do not live up to this reputation. Some goats will never give this amount of milk and it will be no bad reflection on their owner's husbandry. In any case does a small goatkeeper even need upwards of 8 pints of milk a day? Unless there is an outlet for her extra milk, a heavy milker can be uneconomic as she will require additional food if she is to stay a healthy animal.

British Alpine kid at six months old

Roughly, goats will divide their intake of digestible nutrients into three equal parts: for maintenance, processing, and the milk. In varying degrees, these three processes need a small proportion of protein and a large proportion of carbohydrate and starch. Their systems need very large amounts of fibrous material to keep them in good working order. On the domestic scene it is highly unlikely that this fibrous material will contain enough protein, and so this must be provided with concentrates. The diet should also include the correct mixture of vitamins and minerals which are vital to the various bodily functions.

Goats will only be as good as the food that they are given so it pays to take a little care when considering their rations.

Hay

The staple part of the goat's diet is hay and they like a good, rough mixture; lucerne, clover, rye grass, and all the other meadow grasses are very palatable; comfrey and nettle hay are of the very highest quality. Cocksfoot grass is not so good, for although it has plenty of bulk it is too wiry – like knitting needles. Mouldy hay should never be given because this could cause chest complaints, if the goats decided to eat it. Pea straw, oat, and barley straw lack the goodness of hay but do provide good roughage and the goats love them. It is very important that goats have a feed of hay before leaving their pens as this will provide warmth as they digest it.

Concentrates

As previously mentioned protein must be provided with a concentrate ration. The ruminant does not process proteins very efficiently, so the grains which have a high carbohydrate content will be better utilized. Crushed oats and flaked maize with the addition of rolled barley and bran, are quite usual. Broad bran would make a meal in itself, but today it is usually cut too finely. A very small amount of soya bean meal, or ground nutcake, can be added (or linseed cake although this might have a laxative effect). In winter a handful of grass and lucerne nuts is a very useful supplement to the ration, whilst soaked sugar-beet pulp will provide some extra bulk and the goats usually enjoy it. Do please note that no more than 6 oz. of pulp a day should ever be fed dry.

British Toggenburg milker

SOME EDIBLE PLANTS

Great Willow Herb
(Epilobium hirsutum)

Dock
(Rumex)

White Horhound
(Marrubium vulgare)

Coltsfoot
(Tussilago farfara)

Wild Strawberry
(Fragaria vesca)

Hogweed
(Heracleum)

Sowthistle
(Sonchus oleraceus)

Rose hips
(Rosa)

SOME POISONOUS PLANTS

Greater Celandine
(Chelidonium majus)

Yew
(Taxus baccata)

Henbane
(Hyoscyamus niger)

White Bryony
(Bryonia dioica)

Foxglove
(Digitalis purpurea)

Ragwort
(Senecio jacobaea)

Deadly Nightshade
(Atrota bella-donna)

Buckthorn
(Rhamnus catharticus)

Spindle
(Euonymus europaeus)

Brassicas, Roots, and Branches

Brassicas are a valuable source of food although an excess could result in an iron deficiency or tainted milk. Those which are most usual for feeding goats are ordinary or thousand headed kale, cabbage, or sprouts. Amongst the usually acceptable root crops are cattle beet, mangold, swede, carrot, and turnip. Goats also like onions and leeks and these are good for purifying the system.

Hedge trimmings and branches are the favourite foods of all and amongst these are elm, chestnut, maple, willow, and ash. Elder should be used only very sparingly because of its strong laxative effect. Prunings from fruit trees are first class, but bark should not be sliced off the trunk because it will kill the tree.

There are brambles and many weeds which are a very acceptable source of food, amongst these are: wild strawberry, blackberry, hawthorn, rose hip, dandelion, sorrel, dock, sow-thistle, harehound, willow herb, hogweed, and plantain.

Certain plants and trees are, of course, poisonous and these must be avoided at all costs, some of these are: alder, yew, laurel, laburnum, rhododendron, ragwort, deadly nightshade, henbane,

Anglo-Nubian milker.

spindleberry, bryony, foxglove, buttercup, and white bryony.

Minerals and Vitamins

Iodized salt mineral licks and cobalt licks should always be hung in the pens. It is now becoming more usual to buy these combined in one white block. Apart from this, there should be no need for extra mineral supplements – unless there is a known deficiency. An excess of minerals is not good and an analogy could be drawn with the oil in a motor car engine; only just enough is needed to ensure that it runs smoothly, but an excess would put wear and tear on the bearings. Also, an excess of one mineral is likely to destroy the beneficial effect of another. If you like there would be no harm in giving herbal tablets as they contain compounds of various plants such as garlic, rue, sage, wild thyme, and raspberry, all of which have health giving properties. A dessert-spoon of cider vinegar a day is said to be a natural conditioner and preventative of everyday animal ailments. Last but not least, water is very important and should be available at all times.

Daily Rations and Timetable

Approximately, a basic daily maintenance ration should include 1 lb. (·45 kg.) concentrates, upward of 5 lb. (2·3 kg.) hay, and 10 lb. (4·6 kg.) vegetable matter. Five oz. (142 g.) of concentrate should be added for each 1 lb. (·45 kg.) of milk yielded. Various combinations of concentrates can be bought ready mixed. Many goatkeepers prefer to mix their own and a sample of this might be four parts oats, two parts flaked maize, two parts rolled barley, one part bran, and one-eighth part soya bean meal.

Hay should not be fed when it is very new as, like new bread, it is indigestible. As kale is very juicy it should be collected the day before it is needed so that it has a chance to wilt. Mangolds and fodder-beet have a high water content and they should be cut and stored until after Christmas so that they can dry out. Remember that when feeding fruit such as apples these must be sliced.

Feeding routines will vary to suit the individual goatkeeper and the following is just a rough guide. Half the days concentrate is given at morning milking; the water is then changed and the hayracks are filled up; in the middle of the morning the goats go out if the weather is fine, but if they have to stay in, or there is not enough forage outside, feed greens, roots or branches at midday and then fill up the hayracks. If the goats are out bring them in one hour before milking. Feed the second half of the concentrate at milking time and check the water. Any and all changes to a goat's diet should of course be done gradually as otherwise there is the risk of an upset stomach.

Growing, Buying, and Collecting Food

It is of course possible to keep goats entirely on bought foodstuffs but it can make the daily 'pinta' much too expensive. A goat garden, where some vegetables can be grown just for them, would be a very great asset. However some foods such as sacks of stock feed roots are to be had at reasonable prices from farmers or market gardeners, whilst greengrocer shops are a likely source of supply as they will probably give you unsold vegetables and other trimmings.

Hay is expensive; if you have a piece of land which you can let grow wild, or cultivate and sow with a herbal hay, it will be an advantage. Haymaking is an art which is dying out but perhaps you could find an old craftsman to instruct you. You would be able to learn of the correct way to scythe the swathe and turn it daily in the sun until it dries, and then to stack it.

An abundance of hedgerow growth is to be had by the goatkeeper who is prepared to spend the time in gathering it. Beware of food from roadside verges which could be contaminated by exhaust fumes, or from the edges of railway tracks which may have been sprayed with weedkiller.

Drying Food for Winter Storage

Collect plants such as branches, hedge trimmings, or weeds which are of good food value when they are in prime condition. Put them outside on a clean surface, in the daylight hours if the weather is fine. When they are dry, store them by laying flat on a slatted surface or tieing them in bundles from beams.

Chapter 6

General Care and Maintenance

Daily Routine

As they are such creatures of habit your goats will feel secure if each day follows as nearly as possible the same routine. The daily tasks should be carried out methodically and with an easy efficiency; any left-over food should be removed and the buckets cleaned. The water should be changed twice daily and, in the winter, the goats like to have it warm. Check that no baler twine has dropped in the pens; the goat is quite likely to pick it up, chew it, and cause herself all sorts of problems. It could become firmly wound round her teeth and actually loosen them as she tries to free it. If it was swallowed it would probably go through her – but it could form a tight ball within the stomach.

Going Out

If you are introducing a new goat into the herd be prepared for sparring when they go out to pasture. This always looks much worse than it is and they should soon settle down to an easy relationship. Nonetheless, it is better to keep horned goats apart as they could cause injury to the others.

The environment to which domestic goats have become adapted makes them susceptible to cold, and they should not go out if the weather is very bad. However, if the day is cold but bright, they should be able to venture beyond the confines of the goathouse if only for quarter of an hour's exercise. As soon as they start to lie down, or they look cold, they should be taken in. They will probably be only too ready to tell you if they find the weather inclement. Here again, the goat on a tether is at a disadvantage because she cannot exercise enough to keep warm. The goats must not be allowed to get chilled as it could result in pneumonia, apart from which any energy expended on keeping warm will be less energy used in milk production.

A goat caught in a sudden downpour should have a brisk rub down with a towel, whatever the time of year. If you have to lead a

45

stubborn goat try not to pull as it will only develop into a tug-of-war; if you relax the lead and walk forward, she will probably follow you.

Grooming

A weekly grooming with a dandy brush and a metal tooth comb should keep the animals' coats in good condition. In winter, goats grow a warm woolly undercoat so beware of over-zealous grooming at this time lest you brush it out.

Hoof Trimming

Once you have learned how, hoof trimming is a simple operation which is better carried out little and often. If hooves are allowed to grow so much that they become hopelessly mis-shapen, it can be difficult to correct, and there is much more danger of footrot. Overgrown hooves can make walking uncomfortable and the young goat could develop cow-hocks. Hoof trimming shears or paring knives can be purchased from farm suppliers, and the former look rather like sécateurs; they perhaps will be more advisable for the beginner to use. Trimming is best commenced when a kid is one month old and then carried out as a monthly routine. The hoof should be trimmed back until it is level with the sole, and then the heel must be levelled. Most local goat clubs will usually lay on a hoof trimming demonstration, so it might help you to see it done by an expert.

Worming and Entero Toxemia Vaccination

These two very necessary tasks should be carried out twice yearly and could be done together. For worming, Thibenzole tablets are safe and effective, and can be purchased from farm suppliers or the secretary of your local goat club. They can be crushed up and added to the goat's food or administered with the aid of a pill gun. The pill is slotted into the end of the gun which is put into the back of the goat's mouth and the pill is shot out with a spring action. The dosage is 1 tablet for an adult goat and ½ tablet for a kid, but the kid should not need worming until she goes out to pasture. An in-kid goat should be wormed seven weeks after service and three weeks after kidding.

Pill gun.

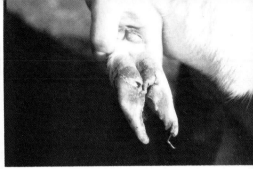

Overgrown hooves in need of trimming

Hooves in need of trimming can cause lameness

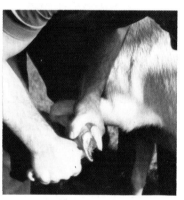

The correct way to trim a goat's hoof

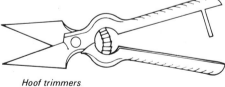

Hoof trimmers

The hoof and sole after correct trimming

Entero Toxemia is a very serious disease, but there is no reason for it to worry you provided that your herd is vaccinated twice a year as a precautionary measure. The appropriate vaccine can be obtained from your vet.

The process of injecting is a relatively simple procedure and, to save vets bills, you could learn to do it yourself. Do seek expert guidance first though and get someone to come and give you a practical demonstration.

Housework

It is obvious that the goathouse must be kept as clean as possible, but in the winter months the bedding can be allowed to build up more. This provides better floor insulation, greater warmth, and urine is more readily soaked up. Fork over the litter daily and add a little more straw as and when it is needed. You will always notice that a goat likes to scratch a bed for herself before she nestles down, so she will appreciate the daily 'plump up of the pillows'. As goats often pull down as much hay as they eat they tend to litter themselves down but this is not a commendable practice – the price of hay being what it is. An advantage of allowing the bedding to build up is that the bacteria get to work and break down the manure underneath, adding to its value for the vegetable gardener. A build up of muck in summer is not a good thing as it will attract flies and, apart from anything else, goats hate flies.

When the pens have been cleaned out they can be washed down with a disinfectant solution such as Jeyes fluid, but it should not be too strong. Over enthusiastic use of strong disinfectant, far from being beneficial, can have a deleterious effect. It will inhibit the growth of the bacteria responsible for the breakdown of the manure and the composting process will not work. The use of strong disinfectant could also be responsible for tainting the milk.

Above all else never allow your goats to become a chore. If you find that the daily routine is becoming an effort, the time has come for a re-think. Have you got too many goats or can you streamline your husbandry? Remember that two animals well fed and cared for are of more value than four poorly kept.

Psychology

The smaller goat owners have an advantage over the breeder of the large herd because they are in a better position to become acquainted with the ways of each individual goat. Too many of us do not spend enough time with our goats just observing their ways. If we learnt a little more of the idiosyncracies of each goat we would soon note any peculiarities of behaviour and thereby detect an early sign of illness.

The Firm Hand

Always be kind, but firm, with your goat and never allow a goat to dominate you; they have an advanced social structure and in the wild they feel safe and secure when they have a leader who can assure a happy and close-knit community with her authoritative air. This is the position that the handler of the domestic herd will have to adopt; if ever you are toppled from this position of headship it will undermine the goat's self-confidence.

Case History

One day, a new owner took possession of a goat who had proved just too difficult for her last owner to manage. That evening, at milking time, a battle of wills commenced as the goat was quite determined that she would not be milked. Each time she jumped forward, sat down or kicked, she was made to stand again by the quietly determined new owner. Eventually the handler triumphed, having milked the goat dry, although she had to admit to being in a cold sweat by this time. The following morning the new owner approached the goathouse with some feeling of trepidation, quite prepared for the battle of wills to recommence. She need not have worried because the goat stood on the milking stall as firmly as a rock. She had accepted the new owner as her herd leader and from that sorry start emerged the most charming animal.

Chapter 7

Breeding and Kidding

by Phyllis V. Minter

Breeding Cycle

It is a fundamental law of nature that all mammals must give birth in order to produce milk. With the domestic animals the milk which is surplus to the needs of their offspring, can be utilized within the household. The primary value of the goat lies in the unique qualities she possesses as a milk producer. Most well-bred goats (apart from those of African origin) will produce milk, without a break, for two years. With two goats and a little careful planning, it is often possible to ensure a supply of milk for the whole year. Each goat can be mated in alternate years and when one is dry, prior to kidding, the other will be milking through. The normal rutting season starts around September, when the nights draw in, and the kids are produced in the spring; thus, the kids have the fine summer months in which to develop. The actual period of gestation is five months. If a goat is not mated in her first heat of the autumn she will continue her cycle until February. Some goats will come into heat earlier than September, and later than February, but these are unusual.

Opinions vary as to what age it is best to mate a goatling, but to a certain extent it depends on the individual animal. A very early kid, who is strong and well grown, could be mated just before Christmas in her first year, though it would be more usual to wait until the second year – when the goatling is between fifteen and eighteen months. Goats have the ability to mate at a remarkably early age but those who breed early do not seem to develop to their full potential. A healthy goat should be quite capable of breeding until she is at least seven, and probably much longer.

Heat

Heat periods occur every twenty-one days and each individual heat is of about two days duration. However, it can be as short as three hours or as long as three days. When you are first aware that your goat is on heat it is better to take her to the male as soon

GESTATION TABLE SHOWING WHEN GOAT IS DUE TO KID

MATED SEPTEMBER / KIDDING JANUARY → **FEB.**

MATED	1	2	3	4	5	6	7	8	9	10	11	12	13	14	15	16	17	18	19	20	21	22	23	24	25	26	27	28	29	30
KIDDING	26	27	28	29	30	31	1	2	3	4	5	6	7	8	9	10	11	12	13	14	15	16	17	18	19	20	21	22	23	24

MATED OCTOBER / KIDDING FEBRUARY → **MARCH**

MATED	1	2	3	4	5	6	7	8	9	10	11	12	13	14	15	16	17	18	19	20	21	22	23	24	25	26	27	28	29	30	31
KIDDING	25	26	27	28	29	1	2	3	4	5	6	7	8	9	10	11	12	13	14	15	16	17	18	19	20	21	22	23	24	25	26

MATED NOVEMBER / KIDDING MARCH → **APRIL**

MATED	1	2	3	4	5	6	7	8	9	10	11	12	13	14	15	16	17	18	19	20	21	22	23	24	25	26	27	28	29	30
KIDDING	27	28	29	30	31	1	2	3	4	5	6	7	8	9	10	11	12	13	14	15	16	17	18	19	20	21	22	23	24	25

MATED DECEMBER / KIDDING APRIL → **MAY**

MATED	1	2	3	4	5	6	7	8	9	10	11	12	13	14	15	16	17	18	19	20	21	22	23	24	25	26	27	28	29	30	31
KIDDING	26	27	28	29	30	1	2	3	4	5	6	7	8	9	10	11	12	13	14	15	16	17	18	19	20	21	22	23	24	25	26

MATED JANUARY / KIDDING MAY → **JUNE**

MATED	1	2	3	4	5	6	7	8	9	10	11	12	13	14	15	16	17	18	19	20	21	22	23	24	25	26	27	28	29	30	31
KIDDING	27	28	29	30	31	1	2	3	4	5	6	7	8	9	10	11	12	13	14	15	16	17	18	19	20	21	22	23	24	25	26

MATED FEBRUARY / KIDDING JUNE → **JULY**

MATED	1	2	3	4	5	6	7	8	9	10	11	12	13	14	15	16	17	18	19	20	21	22	23	24	25	26	27	28	29
KIDDING	27	28	29	30	5	6	7	8	9	10	11	12	13	14	15	16	17	18	19	20	21	22	23	24	25	1	2	3	4

51

as possible, and not rely on her heat lasting for two days. There are several indications of heat which occur in varying degrees of intensity: she will bleat long and loudly and there will be vigorous wagging of the tail; she will have a swollen vulva and a slight discharge; her milk yield might drop and she could also lose her appetite – this is the time to take her to the male. If she will not stand for the male it could mean either that she is not quite ready or, more likely, that you have left her too late. If this is the case you will then have to wait until her next heat and repeat the process.

It is just possible that she might return to heat even when she has stood for service, but a return visit should do the trick. In the unlikely event that she still returns to heat after two matings there might be something wrong and this is the time to seek expert advice. Occasionally a goat, usually young, will have a false heat which means that, after standing for service, she will return to heat after ten days. More rarely found is the goat who repeatedly returns to heat and then kids to correspond with the first date of service. However, do not be daunted because a healthy goat – as no doubt yours is – will be very unlikely not to produce kids from the first mating.

Choosing the Male

It is perfectly understandable that any goatkeeper with little interest in showing, might question the need to be selective when finding a male. As the prime importance of mating is to secure a supply of milk what point is there in bothering about pedigrees? This question raises many more subtleties than are at first apparent, as the resulting progeny must not be overlooked. It is most desirable that stock is produced which is well formed, constitutionally sound, and has a good capacity for milk production. Breeders select only the very best males from proven lines for stud. These males carry in their genes the fine qualities of their dams which they in turn can transmit to their daughters. It is also desirable to breed to type. No dog breeder would think of crossing a Labrador with a spaniel, and still call the puppies pedigree stock, and why should goat owners be any different?

One important point to remember is that two polled goats should never be paired; there is a genetic factor which could result in the birth of hermaphrodite kids.

A list of Stud Goats is published by the British Goat Society each year, around August, and there are also advertisements to be found in local club newsletters. Consider carefully which male is to be used and make sure that, when the time comes, you will have adequate transport.

When your goat shows her first signs of season, contact the

owners of the chosen male so that they know you are on your way and you are ready to go.

Stock Movement Record

As a precaution against disease, it is required by law that a record is kept of the movement of all stock. This need not be elaborate and a simple children's exercise book would be quite adequate.

STOCK MOVEMENT RECORD

DATE	GOAT	MOVED FROM	DESTINATION
15 Aug '78	Abacus Alexis	The Hollies, Little Bealings	Gayfers Playford
20 Aug '78	Abacus Alexis	Gayfers Playford	The Hollies, Little Bealings

Kidding

Most kids arrive in this world during the spring, and this is the real highlight of the goatkeeper's year when all the hopes, kept alive through the dark, dreary winter days are either fulfilled – or dashed: it is the time that most new goat owners look forward to with the greatest fear and trepidation. Perhaps I can reassure them to some extent when I say that, in well over 50 years of goatkeeping, I can only remember losing two goats due to complicated kiddings; I have probably not experienced more than ten difficult cases in all that time. The care of the in-kid goat is very important, and she should always have an adequate and varied diet. Variety is the spice of life to all goats, and is especially good for the expectant 'mum' in the short, dull, winter days. The best possible hay, clover, or seeds, if obtainable; a good concentrated mix, some greenstuff or soaked sugar-beet pulp, fed warm should keep her healthy and happy. Some daily exercise is also very important, but it is definitely not advisable to tether out during the winter months. Accidents can so easily happen: a stray dog can worry, unruly children can torment, even a passing car or aeroplane can badly frighten an in-kid goat with disastrous results. A run in a yard or well-fenced paddock – even a walk on a lead along a country lane, is much more advisable. The normal period of gestation in the goat is five months (or twenty-one weeks plus three days, or 150 days, whichever way you prefer to count it), though kids do sometimes arrive up to a week early or up to a week late for no apparent reason, and with no ill-effects on either mother or offspring.

As the end of pregnancy approaches, the goat's concentrated ration should be gradually increased to prepare her for the demands of the coming lactation. I am not a believer in a great deal of 'steaming up', but I do like to have my goats in reasonably good condition before they kid; they do lose flesh very rapidly once they start milk production, especially if they are heavy-milkers.

Milking Before Kidding?

One problem which can arise, particularly with goats bred for high milk production, is when the udder fills up before the kids are due, it is always difficult to know just when to milk, and how much to take. Although I do not like milking before kidding, if the udder seems tight and uncomfortable it really is best to relieve it by taking some. About ten days before the kids are due clean out the pen; if possible scrub and disinfect the woodwork, remove any buckets (particularly water pails), and allow the goat to be loose.

Signs to watch for

As time for kidding approaches the goat will be restless and uneasy; the udder fills up rapidly and will often look tight and shiny; the bones around the tail slacken and the vulva looks full and swollen. Goats are very individual and vary a great deal in how they behave at kidding time. Some show symptoms days in advance – others only a few hours before. Last spring, on a Saturday night, I shut a goatling up which did not show any real signs of impending kidding; she still had two or three days to go (or so I thought), but when I opened the door on Sunday morning I was greeted by two almost dry kids.

The Actual Birth

Most goats lie down to present their kids; a number of them will make a great deal of fuss and occasionally scream out, whilst others take it much more calmly. Sometimes the first kid is *preceded* by a water bag (which usually breaks as it is passed, the purpose of this is to open and lubricate the birth passage), but sometimes the first kid is *enclosed in* the water bag. The kid should arrive with its nose resting on its two front feet and, if this is so, should present no real difficulty, although the head of a large kid can cause the mother some distress. Once the head has been passed the rest of the kid will soon follow, and the mother will almost immediately start to lick the kid very thoroughly; the kid will splutter and sneeze, and this helps to clear the air passages and get the kid breathing. If the kid is at all weakly it may need a little help with this; just wipe some of the slime and mucous from the nose and mouth, but one is usually wise to leave things to Mother Nature and only interfere if it is really necessary. The second kid usually follows fairly soon, with very little trouble, and then sometimes a third. Twins are the most usual, with one of each sex, but singles are quite common as are triplets; I have had quadruplets on at least four occasions, and tend to think that these multiple births are usually associated with heavy milkers.

Complications
Most goats kid fairly easily, and without any complications, but it is as well to be prepared for things to go wrong. Legs are sometimes turned back, or two kids try to come together and get mixed up; heads can be twisted and, fairly frequently, one kid comes backwards – particularly when there are three or more kids; this does not usually cause much difficulty, though the birth often takes longer.

You are advised to let your goats get quietly on with the job; just keep a watchful eye on things but keep in the background and let the goat have peace and quiet.

Get Help If Necessary
One should be prepared to seek the assistance of an experienced goatkeeper, or shepherd, just in case the need arises. Call in the vet? Just when one should do this is a difficult decision to make; I do not think an inexperienced person should interfere unless they know exactly what they are doing. Cases of assisted kiddings usually need antibiotics so it is probably best to call the vet early, rather than late. Goats these days are valuable animals, so it is advisable to get help in good time.

Retained Afterbirth
This can occur, particularly after assisted kiddings. The afterbirth should come away cleanly and completely, within a few hours after kidding, but sometimes membranes are left hanging, and this shows that the 'cleansing' has not been complete. Again it is not easy to decide just when veterinary advice should be sought; if the goat is eating well, it can be left for up to twenty four hours and I have had a goat pass the afterbirth two days after kidding, without any assistance, and with no ill effects. But all things considered it is probably better to err on the cautious side and seek expert advice early rather than late as Metritis (inflammation of the uterus) can result, and this can be a lengthy business to clear up, with a ruined milk-yield probably for a large part of the goat's lactation.

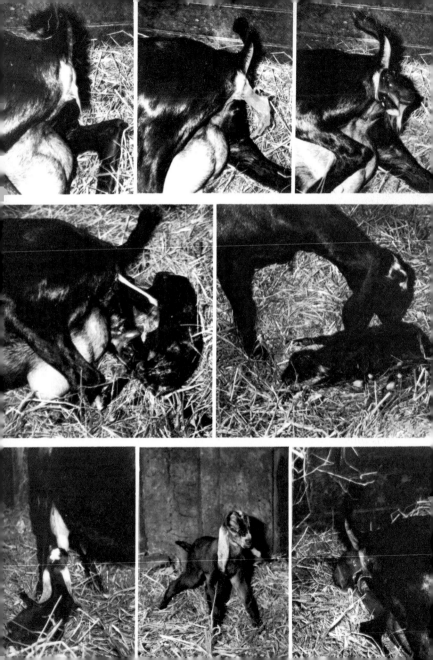

THE BIRTH OF TWO GOATS
A commentary by Clifford Fairhurst

The first signs that labour had commenced was a mucus discharge at the vulva and the doe pawing the bedding.

The second stage of labour started with the rupturing of the amniotic sac followed three minutes later by the first contraction lasting twenty seconds and presenting hoof, and head.

After a rest of twenty seconds the second contraction resulted in the presentation of the full head and shoulders. There followed a further four contractions – the final one being the shortest and completing the birth – the umbilical cord still attached. As the doe stood up the stretching action on the cord severed it sealing both ends thus preventing haemorrhage. When the kid was free from the doe she began cleaning it during which time the kid made its first attempt at standing and began rooting for food. With a little assistance the kid was suckling just five minutes after its birth.

As the second birth was now imminent the kid was placed in a safe place to one side of the stall. The second birth was completed in four minutes with only three contractions. During the cleansing of the second kid the afterbirth or placenta was expelled.

Both kids making a supreme effort but without human assistance took a long feed.

If goats can show any emotion then this one did, and it can only be described as one of absolute delight. During the confinement the doe had tended to be nervous, now all was well. The whole event took just over one hour.

Aftercare

The afterbirth is usually passed an hour or so after kidding, and should come away cleanly, leaving no strings or membranes hanging. Although the goat will usually eat it (if left to her own devices), it is best to remove it in an old bucket and either bury or burn it, as it can be rather indigestible stuff. The goat will by now be ready for a long, warm drink. Some people add oatmeal though my goats never seem to appreciate this and prefer a good dollop of treacle, black for preference, or sometimes I just add salt. One is often advised to give a warm bran mash after kidding but again I have never found this to be much appreciated.

The pen should be tidied up, clean straw put down, and a little milk taken from the mother and offered to the kids in a warmed bottle with a lamb teat. Then the whole family should be left to settle down and have a nice rest. Feed the best hay possible – try to reserve a little for this purpose – some varied greenstuff, and only a limited amount of a light concentrated ration for the first few days after kidding, then gradually bring the goat back to her full concentrates.

Do not milk out completely for at least the first forty-eight hours after kidding or the goat may run the risk of milk-fever; this is caused by the sudden loss of calcium, of which the first milk contains a great deal. The kids can stay with their mother for the first four days, after which you must make up your mind what is to be done with them. Do not keep male kids unless they are really well-bred as the demand for males is always very limited. Only a few people wish to, or are able to, keep stud males. Please, never give them away as pets. Almost always they end up as very unwanted, and sadly neglected animals; they grow big, rough, and very smelly by the time they are six months old.

Female kids too should be carefully scrutinized to make sure they are sound, sturdy, and free from defects such as double teats, twisted faces, over or undershot jaws. Rearing kids is a costly business these days and therefore it really does pay to rear only sound, well-bred stock. If you intend to bottle-feed the kids they should be separated from their mum on the evening of the fourth day. I prefer to put them into an adjoining pen where mum can see, and even sniff them, but they cannot suck from her; neither mother nor offspring seem to miss each other like this. The kids are fed four times a day, with their mother's milk to start with (this to be as near blood heat as possible). The kids can be left on the mother and reared naturally if preferred, but this has many snags: the kids will probably take nearly all the milk – so one gets little for oneself; you have no idea what sort of yield the goat is

Anglo-Nubian and Toggenburg kids.

giving; and when the eventual parting time does come, separating the dam from the offspring can present many problems.

Disbudding

Horned kids can usually be detected at birth by the two small bumps where the horns will grow, as opposed to the completely smooth head of the naturally hornless kid. Also the hair often curls round the horn buds of the horned kid. It is definitely inadvisable to allow a kid to grow up with horns, however docile the animal is, for they can do untold damage to both people and other goats with their horns, even if not intentional. I know of one man who had his wrist broken by a goat catching his hand between its horns, and suddenly twisting its head.

My own kids are always disbudded by a reliable vet who has

been doing this for over ten years. He likes to have them at about four days old after which he thinks it is less easy to get a good result. The kids are taken to his surgery, usually in the early afternoon, and are given a general anaesthetic by an injection into a foreleg vein; they are disbudded with a hot iron and the results have been very satisfactory. The kids come home, usually waking up by the time they arrive, and although they are a little wobbly for a while, they will take a bottle of milk and really show no signs of discomfort, unless they actually touch their heads against something. The scabs come off about six weeks later, and the hair soon covers the scars.

Some goatkeepers do disbud their own kids quite satisfactorily, but I prefer to leave it to the professionals. Some vets, however, are inclined to be more experienced in de-horning calves, and do not seem to realize that the horn-growth in goats is much stronger than in cattle, and therefore more care is needed to make a good job.

After-Kidding Discharge
It is quite usual for a freshly-kidded goat to have very little discharge for the first few days after kidding and then, about a week later, start quite a copious discharge. This usually worries beginners a great deal but is nothing to get alarmed about. It usually lessens gradually, and clears up altogether in about three weeks; keep the tail as clean as possible – it sometimes helps to clip off the long hair down each side of it.

Chapter 8

Milking and Milk Value

Goats have the unique quality of long lactation, and have been selectively bred to encourage this. Indeed, they have become so adept in this sphere that, quite contrary to a fundamental rule of nature, a 'maiden milker' can sometimes be found; this is a goatling who will yield milk before she has produced young. The milk is an extra bonus for her owner as it is quite as good and wholesome as any other. When she is served she will dry up in the usual way prior to kidding.

Lactation

The lactation period is usually of about thirty-seven to forty-eight weeks duration, but this is governed to a considerable degree by the age and breed of the animal. The actual yield of milk is also subject to the same variations: it is usually between six and eight pints shortly after kidding, and it falls to about three to four pints in the winter. The yield reaches its height in the eighth to twelfth week, and most goats reach their maximum yield per lactation in the second or third lactation. These are only

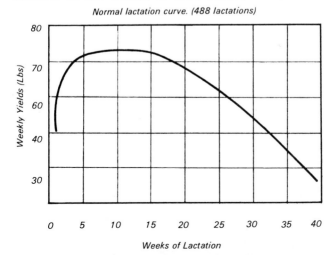

Normal lactation curve. (488 lactations)

Weeks of Lactation

approximations and sometimes yields and lengths of yields will vary more than this.

Milk Recording

As a general guide to the potential of your stock it is interesting to record the individual yields. In addition this could be a guide to the efficiency of your feeding practice, and it could also be an early indication of possible illness. Each time you milk the yield can be weighed and the amount written down. The British Goat Society issues milk recording books for the goat owner's unofficial use, though an exercise book could quite well be used for this.

With the more serious aim of obtaining awards the goats can be milk recorded officially. The British Goat Society operates a scheme in conjunction with the Milk Marketing Board and you can apply to the British Goat Society for more information. The small goat owner may feel that it is too expensive.

TYPICAL MILK RECORD SHEET
Month MAY

	Morning		Evening		Total	
Date	lbs.	ozs.	lbs.	ozs.	lbs.	ozs.
1	5	1	4	15	10	–
2	4	15	4	13	9	12
3	4	14	4	12	9	10
4	4	13	4	12	9	9
5	4	11	4	13	9	8
6	4	10	4	15	9	9

Milking Facilities

Not everyone is so lucky to have a separate milking parlour, so if you have to milk within the goathouse it is most important that each goat is milked outside her pen. The dust in the air is teeming with potentially harmful bacteria, but it just could not be any other way. Every time the goat stirs her bedding, she sets up a fine spray of dung dust and her hairs will float about in the atmosphere. All you can do is to pay as much attention to hygiene as is possible.

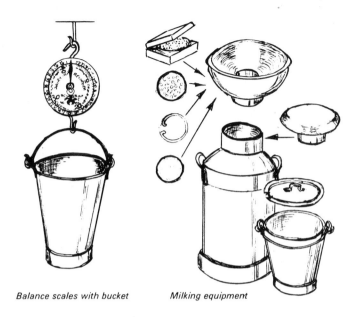

Balance scales with bucket   *Milking equipment*

The milking stall should be kept well scrubbed or at least always covered with a piece of protective paper, during milking, which can be discarded after use. Old paper feed sacks are very useful for this purpose as one layer of paper can be ripped off each time. The walls and the floor should be kept well scrubbed, but on no account must the floor be swept immediately prior to milking. The dust which is sprayed up by the action of sweeping will take about two hours to settle. The next consideration is the mode of dress for the operation; in summer a regularly washed overall would be ideal, otherwise, assuming that your hands and arms are well washed, you can turn back your sleeves to above the elbow. This creates something of a problem in the winter when the thought of baring any part of the body is somewhat daunting. This could be overcome by making elastic cuffs large enough to fit over an overcoat. It goes without saying that you must never milk in your mucking-out gear.

Milking Equipment and its Maintenance

The equipment need not be elaborate so long as it is easily sterilized. You will need a milking pail with a lid and a means of straining the milk into a suitable receptacle. For the pail, tin is the most commonly used material and a home-made strainer can be fashioned with a single-layer piece of kitchen roll laid in a kitchen sieve. Items of dairy equipment can be bought from farm or dairy supply companies and it is better to have these if you can. After straining, the milk must be cooled quickly and small containers can stand in cold water in the sink. If the water is allowed to run, obviously the milk will cool more quickly. For larger amounts of milk some more specific cooling arrangements will have to be made. You could advertise in the press for an inchurn cooler as sometimes dairy farmers have these left over from pre-Milk Marketing Board days, or you could try making your own.

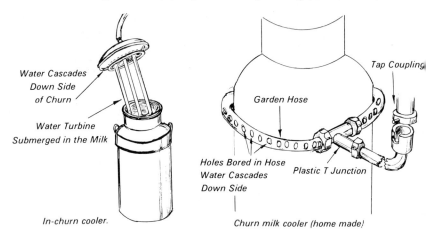

Water Cascades
Down Side
of Churn

Water Turbine
Submerged in the Milk

In-churn cooler.

Tap Coupling

Garden Hose

Holes Bored in Hose
Water Cascades
Down Side

Plastic T Junction

Churn milk cooler (home made)

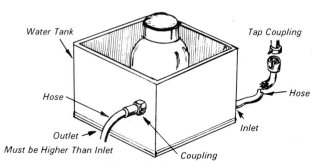

Water Tank

Tap Coupling

Hose

Hose

Outlet

Inlet

Must be Higher Than Inlet

Coupling

Home made churn cooler.

A dairy sterilizing agent will be needed and this can also be purchased from farm or dairy supply companies. All equipment must be rinsed out in cold water immediately after use; they must then be washed thoroughly in hot water with a cleansing agent (washing-up liquid) and sterilizer; they are left to drain until needed next time when they are rinsed out in hot water.

The Milking Technique

Milking commences in earnest when the goat and her kids are separated, four days after birth. Prior to this, all that is usually needed is for the udder to be eased and the kids will do the rest. From the fourth day, the goat is milked twice a day and always at regular intervals. There should be a calm atmosphere in the goathouse although a quietly playing radio should do no harm.

Opinions vary as to whether the goat should be fed as she is milked, but it is very largely a question for the goat and her owner to decide between them. Great care must be taken to milk to the last drop, for if the udder is not milked out Mastitis could be the result. Quite apart from this, the last milk is doubly as good as the first – this is because it holds the butterfats. A further reason for complete milking is that unless you remove all of the milk, the goat will consider that you – her kid substitute – do not need that amount and so will secrete less.

Before milking commences, you should dip a clean cloth in very hot water and ring it out really well. The underpart of the udder is then wiped not only to clean it, but also to stimulate the milk flow. The first few drops of milk, the foremilk, should then be milked into a separate receptacle. Any germs which have gained entry to the teats from the outside atmosphere will be lurking there. Once milking is underway it should not be halted for any reason as this could cause some retention.

It is always difficult to explain the actual milking technique but it is really a knack which should be very quickly learnt. I always think of the teats working on the principle of an hydraulic pump, but the actual drawing of the milk is an emulation of the suckling kid. I feel that I can explain the technique no better than an agricultural correspondent in the *Family Economist Journal* 1849:

'Milking should be conducted with skill and tenderness – all chucking and plucking at the teats should be avoided. A gentle and expert milker will not only clear the udder with greater ease than a rough or inexperienced person, but will do so with far more comfort to the goat, who will stand pleased and quiet, placidly chewing the cud and testifying, by her manner and attitude, that she experiences pleasure rather than annoyance from the operation. Goats will not yield their milk to a person they dislike or dread. You take the teat in your palm, enclosing it gradually in your fingers tighter below than above – but not absolutely tight anywhere – a portion of the upper part of the hand – the thumb is uppermost – embraces a portion of the teat, and the whole hand is drawn gently downwards, towards the extremity of the teat, between the thumb and the forefinger; very little practise enables the milker this with ease, rapidity and tenderness.'

Valuable Goat's Milk

'Goat's milk is green and tastes vile', I was confidently advised by an acquaintance.

There should be no basis whatever for such fantasy. If any truth can be attached to this stigma, it is almost invariably the fault of the goat's owner. In rare cases a goat will be found whose natural physiology will make her produce strong milk, but otherwise it is due to bad hygiene or faulty feeding practice. The goat should produce sweet-tasting milk of the highest quality if she is correctly fed. The goat is a clean animal who never picks up dirty food from the ground; she browses the pasture, picking out the succulent shoots and the choice herbage. All the nutrients are absorbed into her system and produced in the milk.

Therapeutic Agent

Unlike cows, goats are unlikely to contract Tuberculosis, Brucella abortis or Meleteuses (also known as Undulant Fever or Malta Fever). Infected cows can transmit these diseases, through their milk to humans and hence the need for such milk to be pasturized. Goat's milk has much smaller fat globules than cows' milk which makes it more easily digestible; some of the allergy producing proteins present in cow's milk are absent in goat's milk. Its value as a therapeutic agent is becoming much more widely recognized and is very useful as part of the diet of sufferers from ecthyma, asthma, hayfever, migraine, ulcers and many other complaints. It is also much more digestible for babies when they are weaned – many dog breeders feed puppies on goat's milk to produce fine, healthy stock.

It would, however, be wrong to regard goat's milk as the panacea for all ills and it should always be used as part of a sensible diet.

If a change to goat's milk has not evoked the miracle cure, the patient is disappointed, but the sufferer from a gastric ulcer will do no good if he continues to eat chips and sticky buns. The person who is allergic to cow's milk must cut out all products of bovine origin. This not only includes obvious dairy products, but beef, gelatine, chocolate and other items far too numerous to mention. Many babies become sensitized to cow's milk when they are being weaned; had they been weaned on goat's milk they would have set up an immunity which subsequently would have allowed them to include bovine products in their diets. As it is so easily digestible it makes double sense for babies to be weaned on goat's milk. Thus, combined with a sensible diet, goat's milk might well be the relief that is needed in a weakly digestion but it cannot be regarded as the wonder cure for allergies. It serves as a substitute for the irritant properties in cows' milk.

Keeping Qualities

Milk is the 'universal food' and so provides an ideal medium for harmful bacteria which must have sustenance and also warmth in order to survive – just like any other form of life. There is no reason why goats' milk should not keep quite as well or even better than cows' milk so long as it is properly produced. After milking it is most important that the milk is cooled quickly to retard the growth of bacteria.

Disposable milk cartons should never be used a second time as it is impossible to sterilize them properly. Goat's milk can be frozen successfully and this is an enormous advantage as surplus can be stored. It is advised, however, that milk is not left in the freezer for longer than three months.

Outlet for Surplus

Your goats should pay for their keep with the bounty of milk they produce for you, and any surplus could make a little extra profit. You could advertize in your local shop or give your name to the nearest clinic or hospital. Goat's milk is becoming so popular that you might even find people seeking you out first, whether it be for reasons of health or because they just like it. Before you agree to supply anyone, do think ahead to the winter months when yields drop; it is unfair to your customers if you have to let them down. Many owners of larger herds find it significant that there is an increase in demand in winter which drops off in spring.

Chapter 9

By-Products and Recipes

Cheese, butter, and soured milks, are among the earliest foods known to man. Yoghourt is the most simple way of preserving milk and it has its origins in the Balkan countries where it is still a staple part of the diet today. The longevity of some of the Balkan people is attributed to yoghourt. It is only in comparatively recent times that it has become popular in the west, both for its health-giving properties and for use as a very refreshing dessert. Butter, in antiquity, was used as an ointment for skin abrasions more than for use as a food and it is probable that it was introduced to Europe via Scandinavia.

The primitive tribes of Asia made the earliest cheese when they left surplus milk in the sun to sour; when it separated they scooped off the curd. Later, cheese with better keeping qualities was produced by the addition of rennet to the milk. This enzyme comes from the stomach lining of a suckling animal and has the ability to coagulate milk. This discovery was possibly made when milk was carried in bags fashioned from calves stomachs, in which the enzyme was still active. The ancient Greeks and Romans appreciated the nutritive value of cheese, and it is from the Romans that we have our first references to cooking with cheese. The basic principles of cheesemaking are traditional and have hardly changed since the Roman occupation. Cheese was made in country farmhouse dairies through the centuries until the Industrial Revolution. Then the trend was for the country people to move to the towns and, in the middle of the last century, large cheese creameries were set up to meet their needs. Sadly, the art of cheesemaking has largely died out, but there still exists a small farmhouse industry whose cheeses are still to be found on the market. Small goat owners with a surplus of milk are in the unique position of being able to relearn these skills.

Once the simple, basic techniques have been mastered it is largely a matter of experience which determines the good cheesemakers.

If your first efforts are not successful, what you produce can probably still be used for cooking and you have a little more experience for next time. All your equipment can be bought from dairy supply companies although quite a lot of utensils can be found in the kitchen and, with a little ingenuity you can fashion your own moulds. You do not have to have a dairy but there are some points to remember when working in the kitchen: you should never make cheese and yoghourt at the same time; neither should you make bread, stew fruit, or have wine fermenting when making cheese – the different yeast enzymes react unfavourably and spoil the cheese.

You will always need to have plenty of hot water on tap as cheesemaking creates a lot of greasy washing up. All your equipment must be freshly sterilized as undesirable bacteria can multiply rapidly and spoil the end product; have all your equipment in a large saucepan of simmering water on the stove; as you work each item can be taken from the saucepan with a pair of tongs when it is needed.

Cream and Butter

The simple method of obtaining cream is to set the milk in a shallow bowl. When the cream has risen to the top it is skimmed off with a cream skimmer. This is not so efficient as using a separator as some of the cream is left behind. Separators can be bought new, or you could try advertising for a second hand one. For buttermaking put the cream in a large bowl and add each new days cream. The cream must be allowed to mature and after four days, but under a week, the butter can be made.

You will need:
1 kitchen sieve
1 pair of Scotch hands (butter pats)
1 wooden board
1 dairy thermometer
An electric mixer or a butter churn
Heat the cream to 60°F and then churn or beat it. When it

Shallow pan and cream skimmers.

69

separates into buttermilk and large granules, stop beating and test the temperature. Pour off the buttermilk and save for baking. Add water at 20°F less than the temperature of the butter granules. Stir round and drain. Now add water again at 20°F less temperature than that of the butter granules. This time pour off the water and drain the curds through a sieve. Turn onto a wooden board and sprinkle with salt at approximately 1 teaspoon to 1 lb. (·45 kg.) of butter. Next work with the butter pats to remove excess moisture, mopping with a clean cloth as you work, then pat the butter into shape and it is ready to use.

Note: to sterilize the butter pats and wooden board soak in cold water, scald in boiling water, and then soak again in cold water. Never use detergent for wooden implements.

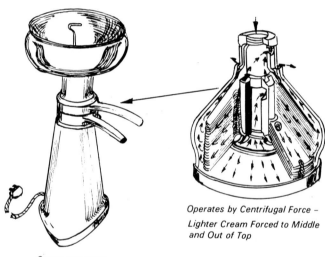

Operates by Centrifugal Force –
Lighter Cream Forced to Middle and Out of Top

Cream separator.

Yoghourt

    1 pint milk
    1 carton yoghourt (unpasturized)
    1 flask
    1 saucepan
    1 dairy thermometer

Butter making equipment.

Heat the milk to 190°F; cool quickly to 115°F. Pour ¾ pint milk into flask; mix 1 tablespoon of yoghourt into the remaining milk and then mix into the flask. Leave for four hours by which time it should be set. Unscrew the lid and leave in a cool place for a further 12 hours before using. Save a little for your next propagation (can be carried on idefinitely but best to discard after a month and start again).

Larger quantities can be made using approximately 4 oz. culture per 1 gallon of milk. Incubate in sterilized ice cream containers. Wrap in blanket and place on top of a boiler or in an airing cupboard. I use the old hay box principle with a bread bin packed with polystyrene chips.

Cheese

To be sure of a satisfactory end product it is best to heat treat the milk to eliminate undesirable bacteria. Unfortunately, it will also destroy the correct cheese making properties. A starter culture will reintroduce these, thus ensuring healthy ripening of the curd. Starter cultures can be obtained from a dairy laboratory and must be propagated regularly. Of course you do not have to use a starter, but it is much safer if you are a beginner as you can be surer of a good result.

Maintenance of a Starter

Having obtained your starter culture boil some medicine or cordial bottles to sterilize them and fill with boiled milk. Put on caps and turn back half a screw. Stand on a trivet in a saucepan and immerse up to their necks in water. Simmer for an hour (ten minutes in the pressure cooker). Take from saucepan and leave to cool at room temperature. Unscrew cap of starter culture and the cap of a sterile bottle and hold the caps in your crooked little fingers. Quickly pick up the bottles and holding over a lighted gas ring (sterile atmosphere) pour some starter into the other bottle. Quickly screw back the caps. Put the bottles into a warm place and leave to activate for 24 hours when they should have thickened slightly.

Basic cheese making equipment.

If you do not wish to make cheese regularly you can freeze culture. Take some half-full bottles of sterile milk, add your starter but do not incubate until after freezing.

For once-only use you could make your own simple starter. Heat some milk in a sterile bottle to 90°F. Crumble a piece of cheese (any variety but preferably soft, not processed) into the milk. Leave in a warm place for 24 hours.

Lactic Curd Cheese

The cheese contains most of the nutrient of the raw milk. It is easily digestible and can form a useful part of an infant or invalid diet. It can also be used very successfully in a wide variety of sweet and savoury dishes. If you do not wish to use rennet, this recipe is particularly suitable for goat's milk and should yield approximately 2 lbs. (·90 kg.) of cheese per 1 gallon milk.

Recipe

    4 pints whole or separated milk
    Salt
    Starter
    1 saucepan
    1 dairy thermometer
    Container to set milk
    Cotton cloth
    Muslin cloth

Heat the milk to 160°F and cool quickly to 90°F. Stir in 1 tablespoon starter – leave in a warm place for 24 hours. Next heat gently to 100°F and leave for half-an-hour; turn into a cotton cloth and hang this up to drain for 24 hours. Salt at this point (it will hasten drainage) and turn into a muslin cloth; leave to drain for a further 24 hours. Any quantity can be made using 2 tablespoons

Draining lactic curd.

of starter per gallon of milk. Use no more than 1 gallon of curds and whey to 1 cloth for drainage. This cheese should be eaten when fresh, though it is well suited to freezing.

Hard Cheese

A delicious highly nutritious cheese with a firm texture. Apart from the modern use of a starter culture it is made to the same basic principles practised in the farmhouse dairy for many centuries. It will yield approximately 1 lb. (·90 kg.) cheese to 1 gallon milk.

Recipe

2 gallons milk
1 large saucepan or bain marie
1 oz. salt
Starter
Rennet
1 cotton cloth and tray
Dairy thermometer
Curd knife (piece of wire which
   can be bent for cutting the
   curd horizontally)
Ladle
Muslin cloth and suitable mould
   (e.g. loose-bottomed cake tin)

Note. For Vegetarians:
Vegetable Rennet
is available from
Dairy Laboratories

Heat the milk to 160°F and cool quickly to 90°F. Add 3 tablespoons starter and leave for half-an-hour. Stir 1 teaspoon rennet into ¼ pint of water. Add to milk and stir gently but thoroughly. Leave in a warm place to set for 1–4 hours. To test the curd touch it with the back of a finger; if the finger comes away clean, the curd is ready. Slice the curd vertically and then horizontally to make one inch cubes. Now heat the curd for half-an-hour to 100°F. If container is to be placed directly over heat, use an asbestos mat. Stir gently with a well-scrubbed hand to ensure even distribution of heat. Leave for half-an-hour for the curd to settle in the whey. Gently pour off the whey, and ladle the curd into the cotton cloth on the tray. Bring up the edges and pull round to form a loose knot. Put on a sloping surface to aid drainage; after a quarter of an hour slice the curd lengthways into four pieces and stack on top of one another. Re-draw ends into loose knot and in another quarter of an hour repeat this process. After a further quarter of an hour re-stack the curds once more, but do not cut. Have ready the mould with the base removed and lined with muslin. Crumble the curd into very small pieces and mix in the salt then pile this into the mould. Cover with the muslin and then the base (or follower) and apply 20 lbs pressure. The following day remove from press. Immerse in water at 150°F for 15 seconds to set the rind. Wrap in fresh muslin and return to mould the other way up. Apply 40 lbs pressure. After another day turn once more and give a final press, then remove from the mould. Bandage with dry muslin and rub all over with softened lard. Put in a cool place and turn daily for three weeks to one month. As it matures the cheese should grow a blue mould which can be either brushed off or washed off with salt water. If your cheese should go wrong, either in the initial stages or when it is maturing use it for cooking. There is a wide variety of recipes which can turn a disaster into a very palatable meal.

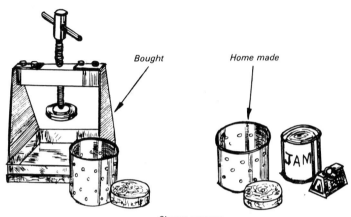

Bought

Home made

Cheese presses

Whey

Do not discard all the whey from the hard cheese. It is a source of lactose and vitamin B and, with the addition of flavourings, it will make a refreshing drink. Use for baking in bread, scones, etc., or try making Gjysost cheese.

Recipe

Reduce about 2 to 3 pints of whey by boiling until it looks caramelly and starts to froth. Remove from heat and beat until the consistency of thick batter. Pour into a small pot.

You can have a whole meal using all that you have produced from your dairy.

French Leek Soup (with lactic curd)

   3 chopped leeks   1 tablespoon rice
   1 large potato diced   3 pints water

Cook until thick. Add 1 tablespoon of margarine, salt and pepper to your taste, and add as much lactic curd cheese as you like. Put this through the blender and you have Vichysoisse.

Hard Cheese and Onion Pie

4 ozs shortcrust pastry	4 ozs grated cheese
$\frac{1}{2}$ lb. onions	$\frac{1}{4}$ pint stock or water
Knob of margarine	Good teaspoon of Marmite
Salt	Freshly ground black pepper
Made mustard	1 egg

Line a 7 in. (18 cm.) flan tin with the pastry. Peel and slice the onions and cook gently in the margarine until soft and transparent. Spread over the pastry base. Spread the grated cheese over the onion. Warm the stock or water and dissolve the Marmite and seasoning in this. Mix in the egg and pour over the cheese and onion. Cook in the oven M.6. Reg. 400°F for about half-an-hour.

Yoghourt Bread and Butter Pudding

4 slices bread (4 ozs)	Butter
Lemon curd	$\frac{3}{4}$ pint yoghourt
4 ozs sugar	2 small eggs
Grated nutmeg	

Liberally spread the bread with butter and lemon curd, and sandwich them together. Put into an oblong casserole dish. Mix well together the yoghourt, eggs, and sugar, then pour over the bread. Sprinkle the top with grated nutmeg. Leave to soak for 15 minutes. Bake M.4. Reg. 300°F for about 45 minutes or until set.

Whey Candy

8 ozs sugar	4 ozs whey
2 ozs butter	Vanilla essence

Melt the sugar in the whey. When dissolved add the butter. Bring to the boil and cook until 238°F or until a tiny piece of the mixture forms a soft ball when put into a saucer of cold water. Leave to cool slightly. Add essence and beat until creamy. Grease a suitable square container and pour in the mixture. When cold, cut into squares.

Kid Meat and Skin

One aspect of goatkeeping that never appeals to many is that it is necessary to put down most male kids. Allowed to grow to maturity, by over sentimental people, they will invariably be passed from one well-wisher to the next and lead a thoroughly unhappy life. Once past the kid stage, and this is very short, they will lose their appeal and become large goats with a remarkable ability to destroy most things they come in contact with. Their offensive smell will saturate everything and even if castrated they will remain a problem.

All too often one sees males almost abandoned, away from the people it was led to believe loved it; he becomes a social outcast. It is better that unless being kept for stud work males should be destroyed at birth or slaughtered at three months of age for meat. In both cases this should be done by the appropriate expert and no one else. At its best, kid meat is rather like lamb. Should you wish to cure the skin yourself then the slaughter-house should be advised of this or you may arrange for the skin to be sent direct for curing to the local hide broker.

Skin Curing (enough for 2 skins)
Take 4 ozs of alum, 4 ozs salt, and 8 pints boiling water. Dissolve the alum and salt in the water and allow to go cold before using. Clean all the fat from the skin and if the skin is dirty wash it well with soapy water and then rinse it well in cold water. Place the skins in the cold solution and leave for thirty-six hours or longer.

If the skins cannot be cured as soon as skinned, stretch and dry in the open air – gently and slowly until time for curing. When ready to cure, steep skins overnight and cure next day. When the skins have been in the solution for the required time, take them out and rinse well in cold water. Next stretch, tack to a board, and set to dry in a suitable shady place. Whilst still damp take from the board and rub well to soften. Do not let the skin get too dry before rubbing or it will not become supple. Once well rubbed, stretch the skin on the board again and rub with fine sand-paper to remove any hard lumps on the skin – but not so hard that holes appear!

Chapter 10

Ailments

I must confess that I find chapters on illness a little alarming, and when I read them wonder if my animals have any chance of survival at all. But, provided that they are properly looked after, there is no reason why animals should not always remain fit and healthy. Nonetheless, it would be wrong to become too complacent and not lose sight of the fact that things do occasionally go wrong, even in the most well-run establishments.

Be Prepared

It would be sensible to assemble a first aid kit, so it is always near at hand in the case of a crisis. This might contain: bandage, plaster, cotton wool, scissors, antiseptic cream, thermometer, udder salve, hydrogen peroxide, glycerine, kaolin, Parrishes food, cobalt salt, garlic pills, a drenching bottle, and a goat coat. In addition it is most important to have the telephone numbers of your local vet and nearest friendly experienced goatkeeper to hand. You can then seek guidance from them without delay if you are seriously worried.

Parrishes Food and Garlic Tablets

Parrishes Food is invaluable when fed to a goat which seems under the weather and off her food. A tablespoon twice daily for two or three days and the animal's appetite returns with a vengeance. Garlic is an excellent cleanser of the blood stream and in my experience the goats always love it.

Cobalt Salt

When they are needed, dissolve half an ounce of the salts in half a pint of water. Pour this solution on to six pounds of salt. 1 tablespoon daily should be sprinkled on the concentrates.

Drenching

Use a longnecked bottle and preferably one made of plastic (to save any possibility of broken glass). Restrict the goat by standing

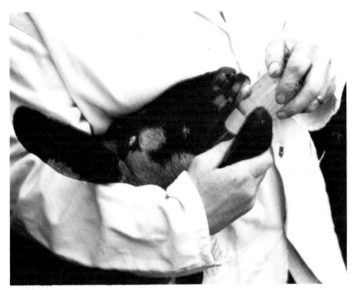

The correct method of administering (drenching) liquids

her in a corner. Stand behind her head and facing the same way. With your near hand, grasp her muzzle and hold your thumb on her tongue. Put the bottle in the corner of her mouth and let the liquid trickle down slowly. If she chokes, remove the bottle and lower her head immediately – if the medicine gets into the windpipe she could well get pneumonia.

Goat Coat

A warm winter coat can be made from an old blanket. A suitable length of strong webbing, with the ends of a leather collar stitched at either end will serve most adequately for the belt and the fastening. Bind all raw edges of the coat to neaten. For a kid coat, the sleeve of an old sweater would be very useful. You could buy some wool or unpick an old sweater and knit one. This pattern is supplied by the British Goat Society.

To fit a one month old kid.
    Materials: 4 ozs of oiled seaboot knitting wool. 1 pair No. 5 knitting needles.

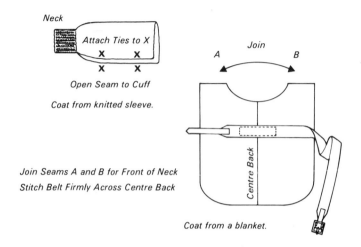

Neck

Attach Ties to X

X   **X**

X   **X**

Open Seam to Cuff

Coat from knitted sleeve.

Join

A   *B*

Centre Back

Join Seams A and B for Front of Neck

Stitch Belt Firmly Across Centre Back

Coat from a blanket.

Pattern: Knitted in two rows. 1st row: K; 2nd row: K.1., P.1. Cast on 60 stitches and K.14 rows pattern.

New row increase 1 stitch each end and every following 10th row (5 times).

Divide to make holes for forelegs as follows:

Knit 12 stitches, turn and knit in pattern increasing on the outside edge in the 5th, 8th and 11th rows, then knit 8 rows decreasing 1 stitch on each row on the inside edge. Slip these stitches on a holder. Join the wool on to the last 12 stitches on the main piece and knit to match, reversing the increases and decreases to match the finished side and place on a holder. On centre stitches knit 16 rows then decrease 1 stitch at each end of the next 8 rows. Pick up the stitches from the holders at each side and knit right across in K.1., P.1. rib for 15 rows, to form collar. Sew up the seams to the end of decreases and the front piece to below the foreleg holes, leaving the collar and rear part of the body open.

To make in Quick Knit wool, cast on 100 stitches and work out increasings to match.

These coats are also very useful for travelling or part of your showing equipment.

Early Warning

As soon as you see that all is not well, act promptly as early treatment might well avert something more serious. The capable goatkeeper is quick to notice if anything is wrong: the goat might be off her food, especially concentrates, and appear not to be cudding; she might be looking miserable and pallid, with her head hung low; her ears might be flopped and feel cold, and she might have watery eyes and nose; her coat might be stary and she might be bloated or scouring.

First Aid

If a goat shows any signs of illness, she should be kept indoors and warm. Do not give her any concentrates but make sure that she has access to some good rough hay. If you can diagnose the problem you may be able to effect a cure yourself, but you can seek the advice of your friendly goatkeeper about this if you need to.

If you wish to take the goat's temperature you can use an ordinary clinical thermometer. This must be greased and introduced into the back passage for 1 minute. If the reading is under 102·5°F or over 103°F you should send for your vet.

The Sick Bay

When the illness has been diagnosed and the appropriate treatment prescribed the goat must be nursed back to health. Unless she has to be isolated she should be allowed to see the normal routine carrying on around her. If she has been prescribed with antibiotics, they may very well be extremely effective. However, whilst destroying the harmful bacteria they also destroy the bacteria within the linings of the stomach which are so necessary to healthy digestion. To reintroduce these you could take half an ounce of yeast and ferment it with a little honey or treacle, and 6 ozs of warm milk and administer it as a drench. Yoghourt is also very good for this and you could offer this to her as she might like it.

As the goat returns to health, try to tempt her with various titbits which you think she might like. A bran mash of 1 tablespoon of treacle mixed in with about 2 good handfuls of bran, and warm water, or milk, is usually acceptable. Perhaps she might like a piece of liquorice plant, some bramble shoots, or a piece of hawthorn. Always make sure that she has fresh rough hay in her rack and do not bother with concentrates until she has recovered. Some of the ailments which are likely to affect goats are detailed in the following:

Acetonaemia

This usually occurs in heavy milkers shortly after kidding, when extra milk production causes the system to become unbalanced. The goat looks pallid and miserable and refuses her concentrates. She might smell of acetone and her droppings look black and sticky. A drench of 4 ozs of glycerine in warm water can be given for three days. A tablespoon of treacle in warm water, or milk, and a course of cobalt salt can also be given.

Anaemia

A gradual lowering of condition with possibly a white discharge from the vulva, it could be caused by a heavy worm infestation. A half a tablespoon of seaweed meal in the concentrate for a few days, a course of cobalt salt and plenty of good rough hay should help. A dose of Parrishes food should be efficacious. The goat should be wormed and kept away from worm-infested pasture.

Bloat

The flanks will be excessively swollen, particularly the left side. This can be dangerous and is probably due to grazing rich wet or frosted grass. Give a drench of 6 ozs linseed oil, keep her walking and massage her sides. If there is no improvement within two hours call the vet.

Chill

The goat looks very cold and miserable with chattering teeth and scours. Probably due to the goat being left outside too long in cold weather, or eating frosted grass and not having had a feed of hay before she went out. Keep her warm with blankets and hot water bottles and give her warm milk and good hay.

Cloudburst

The goat becomes distended as if in-kid. The liquid which is building up in the uterus can be aborted, but it is better for nature to take its course for fear of upsetting the 'heat' cycle later on.

Colic

This causes pain and acute restlessness. It could be caused by poisoning or too much concentrate. Give a drench of 6 ozs of linseed oil.

Contagious Pustular Dermatitis (org)

Spots are seen around the body entrances and these turn into blisters. This appears where the goats are grazed with sheep. The animal must be isolated and the infected parts washed daily with salt water and dabbed with iodine.

Entero Toxemia

A very serious condition which should be avoided by routine vaccination. An infected goat will become strained and be in pain. She will scour badly and lose co-ordination of movement. Convulsions, coma, and death could result in twenty four hours. The vet should be called immediately. A sudden change of diet or too much concentrate or too lush grass could be the cause. The bacteria within the stomach become unbalanced and result in severe poisoning of the system.

Goat Pox

These are spots on the udder which, if severe, can turn into sticky scabs. Scrupulous dairy hygiene should be observed and the udder can be bathed in bicarbonate of soda, mixed to a paste with water, to relieve irritation. Nettle juice is also good to stop itching. Gather some nettles and put them into a bowl; pour on boiling water and allow to steep for a while. This is better when fresh.

Joint Ill

This disease affects the joints of young kids and is usually the result of being born in dirty pens. The germs gain entry through the umbilical cord shortly after birth. The temperature will be raised and the kid will become lame and the infected joint swollen. Injections of penicillin should be given.

Lice

Lice usually affect animals in poor condition. The coat will probably be stary and there will be marked signs of irritation. A good dusting with a proprietary brand powder, as is used for dogs, should be effective.

Mastitis

There are different forms of mastitis. In the acute form the quarter will be hot, swollen, and inflamed. The goat will be off her food, not cudding, and have a high temperature. When it is very severe the quarter becomes gangrenous and the goat could die. The vet should be called and a hot fermentation could be applied to try to relieve the swelling. The cause is possibly from an injury to the udder. Sub-acute mastitis may result in lumps in the substance of the udder. Clots can be seen in the milk and it will probably separate when it is boiled. Intermammary suspension injections are obtainable from your vet and these should be effective treatment. Sometimes the condition will resolve into chronic mastitis. Sponging the udder down with a solution of elder flower and dock is known to be very effective. Gather some elder flower and docks, put into a bowl and pour boiling water over them. Steep for a while and it is best used fresh. Elder flower and dock solution and also nettle solution can be made when the plants are in season and stored in the freezer, in small containers, for possible winter use.

Always observe strict dairy hygiene and milk the infected animal last. Sometimes clots are seen in the milk when no mastitis is present. These could be due to the udder being bruised or can be calcium or solidified protein.

Metritis

This is an inflammation of the womb which usually occurs after an assisted birth or when the afterbirth has been retained for too long. There will be a thick, pink discharge from the vulva and this must be syringed with an antiseptic solution twice a day until the discharge ceases.

Milk Fever

This condition usually occurs shortly after kidding and can be very dramatic. The goat will collapse, her neck will be twisted and she might also have convulsions. The vet must be called without delay. Much of the body's vital reserve of calcium is going into milk production and for this reason a goat should never be milked out completely when she is newly kidded.

Pink Eye (Contagious Opthalmia)

Most commonly encountered in the summer months, when the weather is dry and dusty, the eye becomes cloudy and weeps yellow pus. Dust particles or irritation by flies could be the cause. If not treated promptly, the infected animal could become blind. The eye should be bathed in salt water (about 1 teaspoon to 1 pint boiled water) and pink eye ointment should be applied.

Pregnancy Toxaemia

A faulty concentrate diet in later pregnancy could cause a severe inbalance of the system. The goat looks very miserable; loses her appetite; tends to stagger; and will eventually become comatose. Pour about 2 ozs of boiling water onto 2 ozs glycerine, leave until warm and give as a drench for a few days. Alternatively, glucose injections by your vet will be required. Prevention being the better, ensure the in-kid goat receives extra minerals and carbohydrates in late pregnancy to compensate for the developing foetus.

Tainted Milk

There are several reasons which could be the cause of tainted milk. If it becomes sour very quickly it could be due to inadequate dairy hygiene practice. A bitter taste could be caused by a mineral imbalance such as acetonaemia, or could result from the goat having access to strongly flavoured plants, especially shortly before milking. A salty taste could be the result of mastitis. Lack of cobalt, however, is the most common cause; a course of cobalt salt for seven to ten days should cure matters.

Tetanus

Vaccination should prevent this disease from ever occurring. The germ will gain entry to the body through a wound and this will cause the animal to become increasingly stiff. Eventually the jaws will lock and the animal will collapse (the head is turned backwards in a contorted position and the goat will become comatose). Obviously as soon as there are any signs of this illness the vet must be called immediately.

Worms

There are several different types of worms which are always present to a small degree in any living animal. An indication of heavy infestation is general loss of condition. The twice yearly worm pill should be quite adequate to keep these at bay.

Wounds and Abrasions

Small wounds or abrasions can be treated by cleansing daily with a solution of hydrogen peroxide. Antiseptic cream should then be applied and the wound dressed (a fly repellent powder may also be puffed on after treatment). For more serious wounds you should seek the attention of your vet.

I hesitate to suggest that you might ever lose a goat, but if one of your goats should die, and you do not know the cause, a postmortem should be carried out in case a contagious disease was involved.

British Saanen goatling seen at Suffolk show with her owner Miss P. V. Minter

Chapter 11

Exhibiting

by Phyllis V. Minter

Having started goatkeeping, and one hopes, joined your local goat club, you may very well like to consider showing your goat. Most of the clubs organize at least one show during the summer months; quite often these are for goatlings and kids only, as these are really the easiest to transport and accommodate at a show, but some clubs do cater for milkers too. Most of the county agricultural shows have a goat section and provide covered pens for the animals, usually in a large marquee; these are usually two-day events, and sometimes longer, so they do involve staying away from home for that time, which many goatkeepers may find difficult.

There are also smaller one-day agricultural shows which often provide classes for goats, and these perhaps offer a better opportunity for the newcomer to make a start.

First Steps

Having chosen the show or shows at which you would like to exhibit, contact the show secretary, and ask for schedule and entry forms. Some shows need a separate entry form for each animal, for others you can enter several animals on one form. Do make sure to do this in good time as, especially for the larger shows, entries often close two months or more in advance of the show date.

Do fill in the entry forms correctly, and check, to make sure that you have entered in the class for which the animal is eligible. I know that this sounds very elementary but as a show secretary I do know the mistakes even experienced exhibitors can make, and the heartache these can sometimes cause.

Preparation

The decision to show having been made and the entries sent off, one must now set to work on the animals themselves. Regular daily grooming will help to produce a nice glossy coat; kids especially, should be taught to lead and stand correctly. Careful feeding should be practised to get the best possible condition on the animal, though goatlings in particular may have to be given only a small concentrated ration as they should not be allowed to get too fat and heavy. Keep the pens clean and well-littered to avoid staining, as these are well-nigh impossible to remove once they have been allowed to dry on; any new stains should be washed off as soon as noticed.

A few days before the show the feet should be carefully trimmed and then the animal stood on concrete or other hard surface and checked to see that she stands firmly and soundly on all four feet. Beards should be cut off with a sharp pair of scissors and, often, stained long hair between the fore legs may need a bit of trimming.

Nearly all goats, white or coloured, are much improved by a thorough wash with a good dog shampoo; this makes quite a difference to the texture of the coat, but one needs to be careful with the timing of the wash. When the animals are still carrying their old winter coats this hair will curl after washing, and will not help the goat's appearance. It is advisable to wash, if possible, on a warm sunny day so the animal dries quickly, and avoids the risk of chills. With milking goats always dry the udder carefully and thoroughly. A useful tip is to put a thick, rough towel over the goat after drying off as much of the moisture as possible; cover this with a goat rug, and it is really surprising how quickly the animal dries off.

Arrival Time

As the big day approaches do check from the schedule the correct time of arrival; for the smaller and one-day shows it is usually one hour or a half-an-hour before judging is due to commence, but for the British Goat Society recognized shows, with milking competitions, it is usually about 5 p.m. on the evening before the show. This applies to all milking goats whether entered in the milking competitions or not. Young stock – goatlings or kids – can usually arrive up to about 9 a.m. on the show day, but milkers have to be stripped (milked) under the supervision of the stewards at a specified time, on the evening before, in order that they all start even.

What You Need to Take

Much will depend on the type of show which you are attending. For the afternoon shows you need: collars and leads – strong ones to tie the goats to the stakes (these are usually provided at this type of show) and lighter ones to actually show them on; a net or

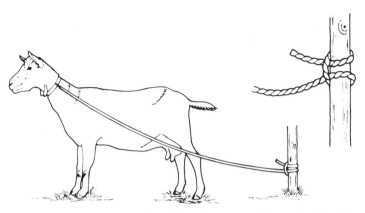

Stakes are usually provided at shows. Ensure that your goat is correctly tethered

Early morning udder inspection at the Royal Norfolk Show (A.O.V. Milkers)

Pure Saanen kid. A Heckington Best in Show winner

bundle of hay; a few twigs or branches to keep them happy and occupied; brushes for a last minute touch up, and perhaps some talcum or dry shampoo powder to cover up any grubby marks.

For a one-day show much the same, with rather more fodder for the goats, a picnic lunch for oneself, a bucket to provide water for goats, kids' bottles (if still young enough to need a midday feed), and a picnic stove or some means to warm the milk – do not forget the matches!

For the larger two-day shows one of course needs much more, and here it is useful to make a list of items required and to tick off as each is packed. For oneself one needs: a camping chair and bed or a lilo mattress; a sleeping bag or blankets (most exhibitors sleep in the marquee near their goats' pens, and most goats seem to settle in much better when they realize that someone they know and trust is nearby. Some people do prefer to sleep in their cars or trailers, where it is usually quieter. Remember it can be quite cold at night, and in the early morning, so take a warm jacket or anorak. Food for self and means of cooking it. Light, warm clothing – as the weather can change suddenly – boots and a good 'mac' are also a must in case of a sudden downpour; finally a reliable torch – groping about in the dark can be very frustrating.

For the goats one needs: buckets for water and food, hay racks, concentrates, hay, green food, for some show straw for bedding, grooming equipment, collars, leads, and do not forget the show passes and exhibit numbers, which are usually sent to you by post before the show.

The Great Day Itself

Do be ready to go into the ring when your class is called, the stewards should tell you how they wish you to line up. Watch your animal carefully, try to have her standing correctly with legs not tucked up under her or stretched out too far, as this may make her back dip. Try never to get between the goat and the judge. It is very difficult to see through an exhibitor when trying to assess an animal's good or bad points. A nice, smart, light collar can sometimes just emphasize an animal's quality.

To do well in the show ring a goat needs to be correctly marked according to her breed standard, of good conformation, with no

British goat. A Newark milk yield winner

Saanen and British Saanen goatling class being judged by Mr. Barber at the Royal Norfolk Show.

really bad faults, and to be shown in good healthy condition, with a nice bloom on her coat.

If, at your first attempt, you finish up well down the line, do not be too disappointed. Try to find out where you went wrong; the judge usually gives some comments on his or her reasons for the placing. Talk to the other exhibitors, most goatkeepers are very friendly folk, and learn by your experiences, and before long you could be walking off with the coveted red rosette.

Milking Competitions

All milking competitions at recognized shows are held under the rules and regulations of the British Goat Society, and the conditions, e.g. stripping out and milking times, are printed in the show schedule – these must be strictly observed. Stripping out is usually about 7 p.m. on the evening prior to the show, and the milk each goat produces in the next 24 hours is what will be judged. The milk is sampled for butter-fat content, and points allotted for yield, butter-fat, and time since last kidding. The British Goat Society has a rather complicated system of awarding stars *, and Q* for goats which reach a certain minimum standard. A goat gaining a total of 18 points, with at least 3·25% butter-fat at each milking, is entitled to a *, and if she reaches 20 points with a minimum of 4% butter-fat at each milking she gains a Q*, the Q standing for quality.

The majority of shows in this country are for female goats, and this is nearly always the case where there are classes for milking goats. The public, even in these enlightened days, are still liable to think that goats smell. It is in fact only the males that smell so it is usually considered inadvisable to exhibit males with milking goats, or at shows where large numbers of the general public are present, in order to play down this image as much as possible.

Male Goat Shows

These are held in various parts of the country in order to give serious breeders the opportunity to assess the conformation and breed points of the various males standing at stud. Because the numbers of males are always rather limited, young stock classes (i.e. goatlings and kids) are nearly always included at these

British Alpine class being judged by Mr. L. J. Garner

Anglo-Nubian male goat 'Northdale Moyse' owned by Mrs. Pat Spring

shows. Sometimes included are progeny classes, which give the opportunity to see the males and the stock which they are siring, together.

Champions and Breed champions

At the larger shows recognized by the British Goats Society, Challenge Certificates for the best male or female goat are awarded by that society, also Inspection-Production Challenge Certificates and Breed Challenge Certificates. To become a champion a male must win three Challenge Certificates under three different judges. A female must win three Challenge Certificates under three different judges and must have gained not less than 18 points on the milking competitions at the same show. She must also have won three Inspection-Production Challenge Certificates with at least 18 milking competition points, and have qualified for a Q*.

Breed Challenge Certificates are awarded for the Toggenburg, Saanen, Anglo-Nubian, British Alpine, British Toggenburg and British Saanen breeds. To become a champion of these breeds a male goat has to win four Breed Challenge Certificates under three different judges. A female goat has to win five Breed Challenge Certificates under three different judges with at least 16 points in the milking competitions at the same shows, and must have qualified for a * or Q*.

Pure Toggenburg goatling with her owner Mrs. Robinson. Photo P. V. Minter

Registration of Stock and Point Scoring

The rules and regulations for registering goats and their entry into the herd book as well as the somewhat complex system of point scoring at goat shows are controlled by the British Goat Society. Readers are strongly recommended to join this society which will supply details of both of these matters (address in Appendix 2). The BGS offers the goatkeeper a complete service for not only does it control registration and the herd book but also issues many leaflets of interest to breeders; a mail-order service further offers posters, calenders, and such items as towels and kid-teats.

Appendix 1

Bibliography

British Goat Society
  Breeds of Goats (by H. E. Jeffrey)
  Dairy Work for Goatkeepers (Freda Yorke 1973)
  Goatkeeping
  Life Story of a Goat

Devendra C. & Burns M.
  Goat Production in the Tropics, Commonwealth Agric. Bureau

Downing, Elizabeth
  Keeping Goats, Pelham Books Ltd, London, 1976

Hetherington, L. U.
  Home Goatkeeping, EP Publishing Ltd, Wakefield, Yorks, 1977

Jeffrey, H. E.
  Goats, Cassell & Co. Ltd, London, 1970 & 1975

Mackenzie, D.
  Goat Husbandry, Faber & Faber Ltd, London

Salmon, Jill
  The Goatkeeper's Guide, David & Charles Ltd, Newton Abbot, Devon, 1976

Singer, A. & Street, L.
  Backyard Dairy Book, Prism Press, Dorchester, Dorset

In addition to the above works the MAFF (Ministry of Agriculture Foods & Fisheries) publish a number of useful leaflets including the following:

Clotted Cream (AL 438)	*Hand Cleaning of Dairy*
Cream (AL 495)	*Equipment* (AL 422)
Cream Cheese	*Soft Cheese* (AL 458)
Dairy Goatkeeping (AL 118)	*Taints In Milk* (AL 322)

MAFF Publications, Tolcaine Drive, Pinner, Middlesex.

Appendix 2

Useful Names and Addresses

Clubs and Associations

The British Goat Society, Rougham, Bury St. Edmunds, Suffolk
American Dairy Goat Association, P.O. Box 186, Spindale,
    N. Carolina, 28160, USA
Goat Breeders Society of Australia, P.O. Box 4317, G.P.O. Sydney
    2001, NSW
Canadian Goat Society, R.R.1., Ormstown, Quebec

Magazines

The Monthly Journal; The Year Book; The Herd Book, British Goat
    Society
Practical Self-sufficiency, Board Leys Pub. Co., Widdington,
    Saffron Walden, Essex
Dairy Goat News Print & Pub. Co., Golden Grove, Llysdy, Bishops
    Castle, Shropshire

Suppliers

Appliances
    Fred Ritson, Goat Appliance Works, Longtown, Carlisle
    CA6 5LA
    Small Scale Supplies, Widdington, Saffron Walden, Essex
    CB11 35P

Rennet & Cheese Cultures
    Christian Hansen Lab. Ltd, 476 Basingstoke Rd, Reading
    RG2 0QL

Cider Vinegar
    Merrydown Wine Co. Ltd, Horam Manor, Heathfield, Sussex

Herbal Pills & Tonics
    Natural Rearing Products, The Hall, Kettlebeston, Ipswich,
    Suffolk

Cheese Moulds
    W. N. Boddington & Co. Ltd, Horsmonden, Kent TN12 8AN

Dairy Thermometers
Astell Laboratory Services Co, 172 Brownhill Rd, Catford, London SE6 2DL

Goat Milk Cartons
Bowater Perga, Princes Way Estate, Gateshead

Mineral Mixtures
Boots Farm Sales, Thane Rd, West, Nottingham, Notts.

Appendix 3
List of Illustrations

Index